Crosscurrents/ *Modern Critiques*
Third Series

Edited by Jerome Klinkowitz

Regina Weinreich

The Spontaneous Poetics of Jack Kerouac
A Study of the Fiction

Southern Illinois University Press
CARBONDALE AND EDWARDSVILLE

Copyright © 1987 by Board of Trustees, Southern Illinois University
All rights reserved
Printed in the United States of America
Edited by Curtis L. Clark
Designed by Design for Publishing, Inc.
Production supervised by Natalia Nadraga

Library of Congress Cataloging-in-Publication Data

Weinreich, Regina, 1949–
     The spontaneous poetics of Jack Kerouac.

     (Crosscurrents/modern critiques/Third series)
     Bibliography: p.
     Includes index.
     1. Kerouac, Jack, 1922–1969—Criticism and
interpretation. I. Title. II. Series: Crosscurrents/
modern critiques. Third series.
PS3521.E735Z95   1987   813'.54   86–13870
ISBN 0–8093–1306–5

Chapter 2 and the section of chapter 4 entitled "Synaesthesia,
Synchronicity, Syncopation" appeared in different versions
in the Kerouac/Pinget special issue of the *Review of Contemporary
Fiction* 3 (Summer 1983): 75–82, 64–68. Copyright 1983 by the
Review of Contemporary Fiction.

For my parents
Pola and Sinaj Weinreich

Contents

Crosscurrents/
Modern Critiques/
Third Series

IN THE EARLY 1960s, when the Crosscurrents/Modern Critiques series was developed by Harry T. Moore, the contemporary period was still a controversial one for scholarship. Even today the elusive sense of the present dares critics to rise above mere impressionism and to approach their subject with the same rigors of discipline expected in more traditional areas of study. As the first two series of Crosscurrents books demonstrated, critiquing contemporary culture often means that the writer must be historian, philosopher, sociologist, and bibliographer as well as literary critic, for in many cases these essential preliminary tasks are yet undone.

To the challenges that faced the initial Crosscurrents project have been added those unique to the past two decades: the disruption of conventional techniques by the great surge in innovative writing in the American 1960s just when social and political conditions were being radically transformed, the new worldwide interest in the Magic

Realism of South American novelists, the startling experiments of textual and aural poetry from Europe, the emergence of Third World authors, the rising cause of feminism in life and literature, and, most dramatically, the introduction of Continental theory into the previously staid world of Anglo-American literary scholarship. These transformations demand that many traditional treatments be rethought, and part of the new responsibility for Crosscurrents will be to provide such studies.

Contributions to Crosscurrents/Modern Critiques/ Third Series will be distinguished by their fresh approaches to established topics and by their opening up of new territories for discourse. When a single author is studied, we hope to present the first book on his or her work or to explore a previously untreated aspect based on new research. Writers who have been critiqued well elsewhere will be studied in comparison with lesser-known figures, sometimes from other cultures, in an effort to broaden our base of understanding. Critical and theoretical works by leading novelists, poets, and dramatists will have a home in Crosscurrents/Modern Critiques/Third Series, as will sampler-introductions to the best in new Americanist criticism written abroad.

The excitement of contemporary studies is that all of its critical practitioners and most of their subjects are alive and working at the same time. One work influences another, bringing to the field a spirit of competition and cooperation that reaches an intensity rarely found in other disciplines. Above all, this third series of Crosscurrents/Modern Critiques will be collegial—a mutual interest in the present moment that can be shared by writer, subject, and reader alike.

Jerome Klinkowitz

Preface

I HAVE WRITTEN THIS BOOK out of my belief in Jack Kerouac's artistry. However anyone may judge it, his writing contributed to a change in the American consciousness. If the immediate impact of *On the Road* could be attributed merely to a superficial fascination with hipsters, wanderlust, sex, and drugs—the usual trappings of Beat literature—that fascination would not sufficiently explain the continued interest in Kerouac today. His work is in demand; it is translated for markets abroad and republished for a widening American audience. Unlike those of many authors of his era, his books will continue to be read. Only the power of Kerouac's language could sustain this interest over the more than twenty-five years since *On the Road* made its initial appearance.

Ironically, the sensational aspects of the Beat myth still prevail over the imaginative process by which Kerouac turned his life into fiction. The secondary literature on Kerouac is mainly biographical. Since Kerouac's death in 1969, six full-scale biographies have told his story.[1] Despite the interest in his life and the popularity of his work, the impact of Kerouac's writing on American literature has been felt but not absorbed.[2]

The critical material useful in the development of my own study has been delineated clearly in the text, notes, and bibliography. Though my main arguments build upon the secondary material up to 1981, I am aware of the more recent studies and have included reference where appropriate. As yet, however, Kerouac's stylistic inventiveness throughout his entire oeuvre has not been examined systematically in a full-scale study. This volume aims to fill that need.

However revolutionary Kerouac's work may have seemed at the outset, he inherited a distinctly American tradition that began as early as Emerson and Whitman. Kerouac's antecedents, though, must be linked to the literary expression of this century as well, in particular to the autobiographical nature and "loose style" of such writers as Thomas Wolfe and Henry Miller and to the adventure themes of such authors as Jack London (who writes about a hobo traveler in his 1907 *The Road*) and Ernest Hemingway (whose rendition of the events in Paris in the twenties as told in his 1964 *A Moveable Feast* is accepted as "fiction"). All these antecedents rely heavily on the mode of autobiography that anticipates the New Journalism. The "loose style" suggests an expansive notion of form that can be seen in the large triptychs of Theodore Dreiser and John Dos Passos. The poetic sequence—particularly those works from *Leaves of Grass* (1855) to *Paterson* (1946) and beyond to which sections can easily be added—further suggests that a writer's entire opus can be viewed as "ongoing" or, in fact, "one book." To this American tradition belongs Kerouac's "one vast book," his Legend of Duluoz.

Acknowledgments

I WISH FIRST OF ALL to acknowledge my special gratitude to Perry Meisel, whose brilliant intuitions guided this project at its earliest stages, to Nina Sydney Weinreich, who inspired this work during her first year of life, and to my husband, Bob Salpeter, who patiently sat through it with me to the end.

In various ways, the following people have also assisted me: James Grauerholz, Ruth Heber, John Kuehl, David Lahm, Janet Lawson, Dave Liebman, Stewart Meyer, Barry Miles, Bob Rosenthal, Rick Salpeter, James Tuttleton, Catherine Warnow, and the late Ahmed Yacoubi.

Further thanks are owed to those who have shared their insights on Kerouac with me: David Amram, Paul Bowles, William Burroughs, Robert Creeley, Allen Ginsberg, John Clellon Holmes, Seymour Krim, Dennis McNally, Gerald Nicosia, and John Tytell.

Portions of the following books are reprinted by permission of The Sterling Lord Agency, Inc.
1) *The Town and the City* copyright © by John Kerouac, © 1978 by Stella Kerouac

A Note on Texts

A S THERE ARE NO STANDARD EDITIONS of
the works of Jack Kerouac, I have chosen the most
easily obtainable texts for the purposes of references
and citations. The following works are cited. Each here
is preceded by its dates: brackets enclose the date of
completion as recorded in Ann Charters's chronology;
the date of publication follows. Each work is then followed by the abbreviation used to identify quotations
from it throughout the discussion.

[1946–49], 1950	*The Town and the City.* New York: Harcourt Brace Jovanovich.	*TC*
[1948–56], 1957, 1959	*On the Road.* New York: Viking.	*OR*
[1951–52], 1974	*Visions of Cody.* New York: McGraw-Hill.	*VC*
[1956, 1961], 1965	*Desolation Angels.* New York: Putnam's.	*DA*
[July 1952], 1959	*Dr. Sax.* New York: Grove.	*DS*

[Jan. 1956], 1958   *Visions of Gerard*. New York:
McGraw-Hill.   *VG*

[Oct. 1953], 1958   *The Subterraneans*. New York:
Grove.   *S*

[1955–56], 1960   *Tristessa*. New York: McGraw-
Hill.   *T*

[Oct. 1961], 1962   *Big Sur*. New York: Farrar,
Straus, and Cudahy.   *BS*

[1968], 1968   *Vanity of Duluoz*. London:
Quartet.   *VD*

[1952–60], 1961   *Book of Dreams*. San Francisco:
City Lights.   *BD*

The
Spontaneous
Poetics of
Jack Kerouac

1

Introduction

Till the gossamer thread you fling catch somewhere, O my soul.

Walt Whitman
"A Noiseless Patient Spider"

THE LOOK OF JACK KEROUAC'S writing—ragged and grammatically suspicious—has been used to justify the adverse response his work has so often received. Observers of the cultural ethos out of which Kerouac emerged offer partial explanations. Morris Dickstein identifies the hostility of critics to the Beats' "incipient experimentalism," which, "like most such 'experiments,' had a rich but neglected literary ancestry."[1] Seymour Krim goes further by explaining the revolt of the avant-garde of the late forties and early fifties as one against a prevailing "cerebral-formalist" temper that was shutting new writers out of "literary existence" because both their personal experience and their literary language had been suppressed by the critical straightjacket of post–T. S. Eliot letters.[2]

To get over the anxiety of this restriction, Kerouac had to debunk the norm for prose in the act of writing it. Kerouac says of his own intentions:

I got sick and tired of the conventional English sentence which seemed to me to be so ironbound in its rules, so inadmissable with reference to the actual format of my mind as I learned to probe it in the modern spirit of Freud and Jung, that I couldn't express myself through that form any more. . . . Shame seems to be the key to repression in writing as well as in psychological malady. If you don't stick to what you first thought, and to the words the thought brought, what's the sense of bothering with it anyway, what's the sense of foisting your little lies on others? What I find to be really "stupefying in its unreadability" is this laborious and dreary lying called craft and revision by writers, and certainly recognized by sharpest psychologists as sheer blockage of the mental spontaneous process known 2,500 years ago as "The Seven Streams of Swiftness."[3]

Of course, the main controversy over the quality of Kerouac's prose has always been centered around the basic tenets of his writing philosophy, especially those tenets that preclude the writer's essential control: revision. But Kerouac was adamant about his critical method; his descriptions, published in *Evergreen Review,* state: "—no revisions (except obvious rational mistakes, such as names of *calculated* insertions in act of not writing but *inserting*). And, "Not 'selectivity' of expression but following free deviation (association) of mind into limitless blow-on-subject seas of thought, . . . write as deeply, fish down as far as you want, satisfy yourself first, then reader cannot fail to receive telepathic shock and meaning-excitement by same laws operating in his own human mind."[4] So, incorporated into Kerouac's aesthetic philosophy is the assertion of the value of deliberately un-revised prose—prose representing, ironically, the height of craft.

But spontaneous prose is not new with Kerouac. John Tytell points out precursors in the automatic writing that developed from the experiments of William James and Gertrude Stein at Harvard in the late nineteenth century. But more than following in any direct line from these influences, Kerouac, as Tytell further argues, attacked the concept of revision at a moral level, because it acted as a kind of secondary "censorship imposed by the unconscious."[5]

The literary history of the spontaneity that precedes Kerouac emphasizes the limited control or power of the practitioners of such a mode over the seeming effusion of language. When M. H. Abrams discusses as a basic tenet of Romantic writing the special usage of the "spontaneous" to express the unconscious, he allows for "the supervention of the antithetical qualities of foresight and choice."[6] Even if his sympathies do not extend as far as the Kerouacean example, Abrams suggests that the idea of spontaneity does not preclude the possible imposition of its own restrictions. In American letters, however, the Emersonian definition suggests the infinite possibilities that Kerouac had in mind. In the section of *Self-Reliance* entitled "Spontaneity or Instinct," the American Sublime is called a spontaneity that is "the essence of genius, of virtue, and of life, . . . that deep force, the last fact behind which analysis cannot go. . . ."[7]

That "spontaneity" be subject to rules is indeed a paradox. Moreover, the tendency to fault Kerouac for his spontaneous, unrevised prose is to obfuscate what is really at issue in his writing. Unrevised prose is a methodology that denies the artist's traditional selectivity in favor of another kind of selectivity. For Kerouac, the impulse was to define himself by the more personal forms that told the truth about his experiences, regardless of inherited literary conventions. So the issue remains: what form is that?

Kerouac's writing is an attempt to discover form, not to imitate it, and to discover experience in the act of writing about it, as if the language of the "mental spontaneous process" could expose some human experience as yet unknown simply because no writer had dared to set it down unimpinged by "craft" in the traditional sense. Yet the obvious irony of this stubborn refusal to revise is that any writer as concerned with the revision process as to oppose it so dogmatically must have this method of refinement keenly fixed in his mind.

Both Kerouac's style and his notion of legend in fact evolved out of his scrupulous avoidance of revision in the traditional sense. Kerouac's first novel, *The Town and the City*, written and rewritten in the late forties and published in 1950, was considered a promising first venture in prose, although imitative of the style of Thomas Wolfe.[8] Kerouac reacted profoundly to this critique, and indeed to the anxiety of Wolfe's influence with *On the Road*. Kerouac liked to think his rambling second novel was written in a manner unlike that of any other, in a style and language commensurate with the rhythm and tempestuous speed he found in experience itself. *On the Road* is the exemplary case of Kerouac's conscious break with an unsatisfactory style, his expression utilizing the special techniques he was articulating in his essays on craft.[9] Kerouac's "spontaneous bop prosody"[10] shaped *On the Road*—which was typed on a continuous roll of teletype paper as if it were one long paragraph—as a nonstop statement of an experience that kept moving, the energy of the language bursting through any limitations imposed upon it by our notions of sentence form.

Even when the novel's publication in 1957 (already delayed seven years and heavily revised at Malcolm Cowley's insistence)[11] brought him instant fame and success, Kerouac was distressed and all the more anxious to get the story down right. Hence the revision, published posthumously in 1973 and known as *Visions of Cody,* was conceived to rectify the distortion caused by editorial revision of material in the earlier work.[12] Significantly, this insistence upon further clarification, to get to the truth about things, forced Kerouac's mind over the material again and forces the reader to recognize that by such repetition a stage of revision is already built into the supposedly "spontaneous" prose. Repetition in fact becomes Kerouac's control.

Repetition provides a critical category for the discussion of spontaneous prose. It suggests a double movement in the act of composition, a movement that progresses and repeats at the same time. As Kerouac wrote spontaneously, the elements of past experience were revised in the act of being recorded. Kerouac's legend-making material is a product of the details of his life repeated in each book. But the recurrence of the past does not only define the design of the legend as a whole, showing the relationship of each novel to the next. Recurrence also marks the interior structure of Kerouac's very language so that the pattern of his whole career reflects in large the more microscopic structure of his language from book to book.

The Design of Legend

Kerouac's plan was for a "giant epic in the tradition of Balzac and Proust," even though, as Ann Charters has determined, he could not discover any literary technique that could weld the separate books of his Duluoz chronology into a coherent whole "even if he tried."[13] Charters's assumption dominates most of the criticism of Kerouac as a legend-maker:

He couldn't come up with any literary technique to help him fit all the volumes of the Duluoz Legend into one continuous tale. All he could think of was to change the names in the various books back to their original forms, hoping that this single stroke would give sufficient unity to the disparate books, magically making them fit more smoothly into their larger context as the Duluoz (Kerouac the Louse) Legend. . . . [H]e wanted the books reissued in a uniform edition to make the larger design unmistakeable.[14]

The claim that each particular novel is insufficiently unified within the larger context of the Duluoz legend assumes a definition of legend that is linear and conventional, that demands the coherence of chronology.

Yet if we consider the broadest criteria for legend, Kerouac's work adheres. Legend can be an unauthenticated story from early times, preserved by tradition and popularity, and thought to be historical; a chronicle of the life of a saint; the fame of a person or place; a caption for an illustration or an explanatory description or key to a map or chart; and, in music, a composition intended to describe or relate a story, without words. Even the most superficial reading of Kerouac's individual novels suggests an attempt on Kerouac's part to make

a fiction out of historical events, recounted in an ironically "oral" tradition, to canonize a "hero" through ex-
tensive retellings of his adventures, to recreate graphically
all within a selective geography of America in the language of the oral storyteller. Kerouac's further wish for
a single design to all his fiction appears in a handwritten
note at the bottom of the manuscript page of a poem
entitled "Daydreams for Ginsberg," dated 10 February
1955, prior to the publication of *On the Road:* "But now
I am beginning to see a vast Divine Comedy of my own
based on Buddha—on a dream I had that people are
racing up and down the Buddha Mountain, is all, and
inside is the Cave of Reality—will tell you later—I would
write as above, free prose."[15]

The Language of Legend

This "free prose,"[16] perhaps Kerouac's most controversial innovation in language, links his design with his
method. Usually misunderstood, however, is the term
"free," which in no way signifies an abandonment of
control. "Free prose" is rather like Wordsworth's "spontaneous overflow of powerful feeling," an illusion for
experimentation but more accurately a highly contrived
artifice to contain the exuberance of "natural" speech.
Likening Kerouac's diction to what he calls the "unfulfilled linguistic intentions of the British Lake poets," Tytell claims that Kerouac sought a diction that would be
compatible with the natural flow of the "uncontrollable
involuntary thoughts" he wanted to release.[17] Kerouac's
continued efforts to refine this seeming outpouring of
language defines his legend.

Although Kerouac hoped that his "spontaneous bop prosody" would "revolutionize American literature" as much as Joyce had revolutionized English prose,[18] "spontaneous bop" has musical, not literary, models, especially the jazz that Kerouac and other Beat writers were hearing as they worked—the music of Charlie Parker, Dizzy Gillespie, and Thelonius Monk. In fact, this musical influence explains the unity of the Duluoz legend as well as the unity of particular works, and helps to define Kerouac's achievement as a single work in process over the course of a lifetime.

Kerouac's literary structures are motivated by the same impulse as the structures of jazz riffs—the impulse to perfect a deliberate style that produces the illusion of spontaneity. Albert Murray defines a jazz riff as a "brief musical phrase that is repeated, sometimes with very subtle variations, over the length of a stanza as a chordal pattern follows its normal progression." Furthermore,

riffs always seem as spontaneous as if they were improvised in the heat of performance. So much so that riffing is sometimes regarded as being synonymous with improvisation. But . . . not only are riffs as much a part of the same arrangements and orchestrations as the lead melody, but many consist of nothing more than stock phrases, quotations from some familiar melody, or even clichés that just happen to be popular at the moment. . . . [I]mprovisation includes spontaneous appropriation (or inspired allusion, which sometimes is also a form of signifying) no less than on-the-spot invention. . . . [T]he invention of creative process lies not in the originality of the phrase as such, but in the way it is used in a frame of reference![19]

This notion of improvisation informs the language of Kerouac's writing at an exact technical level. Though

Kerouac had neither the knowledge of a musician nor the critical vocabulary of a person learned in the subject of music, he clearly demonstrates a profound identification of the creation of music with that of literary works. As he says in his *Paris Review* interview: "As for my regular English verse, I knocked it off fast like the prose, . . . just as a musician has to get out, a jazz musician, his statement within a certain number of bars, within one chorus, which spills over into the next, but he has to stop where the chorus page *stops*." Kerouac goes on to liken the craft of the writer to that of the hornplayer:

Jazz and bop, in the sense of a, say, a tenor man drawing a breath and blowing a phrase on his saxophone, till he runs out of breath, and when he does, his sentence, his statement's been made. . . . [T]hat's how I therefore separate my sentences, as breath separations of the mind. . . . I formulated the theory of breath as measure, in prose and verse, never mind what Olson, Charles Olson says, I formulated that theory in 1953 at the request of Burroughs and Ginsberg. Then there's the raciness and freedom and humor of jazz.[20]

Kerouac thus explains the equivalence of his writing and jazz at the technical level: he argues that his phrasing follows the jazz model; he reveals, in his theory of "breath as measure," his acute care for the sentence, which he otherwise denounces; and, perhaps most important, he acknowledges the control of cadence. The intrinsic elements of Kerouac's writing are therefore structurally similar to a musical motif.

Even when during his lifetime Kerouac's language was mistakenly seen as rough and irresponsible, the critic Warren Tallman understood the sources. In the early essay "Kerouac's Sound," Tallman finds *The Town and*

the City a version of the sentimental music of the thirties
with its strong stress on melody, just as the novel is dom-
inated by its story line. *On the Road,* on the other hand,
illustrates a departure into bebop, "where the sounds
become BIFF, BOFF, BLIP, BLEEP, BOP, BEEP,
CLINCK, ZOWIE! Sounds break up. And are replaced
by other sounds. The journey is NOW. The narrative is
a Humpty Dumpty heap. Such is the condition of
NOW."[21]

Tallman never addresses the questions of how accurately the musical mode could be tied to Kerouac's understanding of narrative language, nor how its interior
structures echo in the exterior structure of the Duluoz
legend. Kerouac went on to describe this musical influence in his essays on craft: "Time being of the essence
in the purity of speech sketching language is undisturbed flow from the mind of personal secret idea-words,
blowing (as per jazz musician) on subject of image."[22]

Perhaps the critic Guy Rosolato in his essay "Voice and
Literary Myth" provides a context for the relationship
between narrative and musical structure: "The musical
instrument . . .—the horn—. . . by its rigid body partic-
ipates in the formation of the sound which traverses
it. . . . One could even imagine a 'narrative' which might
try to maintain itself as near as possible to its own advent
. . . and which would let only its own first moment well
forth. . ."[23] But as yet no critical methodology has
emerged from the musical analogy for the discussion of
Kerouac's work. How, we might ask, do the problems of
a free jazz that is really not free—that is, in fact, structured—apply to the apparent freedom or formlessness
of Kerouac's prose?

The Legend of Language

The very fact that Kerouac's entire literary opus is a revision of an initial story, based loosely on the details of his own life, reveals his intentions for the Duluoz legend. The stages of the mythmaking process bring his art out of the realm of autobiography and into the realm of fiction proper. Since Kerouac is concerned with origins, as are all legend-makers, he depicts the fall of society in a grand design—American as well as Christian[24]—that looks to recapture an original paradise or origin from which all else is a decline.

The early novels, those that reflect the earliest stage of the Duluoz legend, create a paradise of Lowell, Massachusetts, Kerouac's hometown. Similar to other key Kerouac locations, Lowell becomes a geographic location representing the landscape of Kerouac's psyche. The progression of the legend is therefore the literary extension of the "road" metaphor, where experience as travel and hyperactivity reveals the lapsed innocence of this early stage. At another stage, Kerouac will embrace a Buddhist philosophy, an Eastern corrective to his lapsed Catholicism, with the spiritual structure of the quest retained despite his questioning of traditional religious values. Finally, the tragic conclusion of the Kerouac legend is its meditative retreat from society, never quite resolving its egomaniacal—and Emersonian—proclamation of the self, despite the desire for transcendence.

Within each novel though, the legend becomes a repetitive structuring design, a kind of improvisation or solo performance within a given stage of legend. The intended unity of a literary career is thus revealed, though not in the terms of the linear chronology we might expect from mere legend. Kerouac abandons the linear narration of saga for a literary strategy based on the juxtaposition of the images that produce experience, expressed differently at different points in time. Each repetition of events represents them in the "now," in the present, in the truth of the moment—much as a jazzman blows the notes out of a horn, even though, of course, this ideal "now" is itself constituted by temporality. This comparison explains why Tytell's statement that Kerouac never settled for a final form,[25] does not contradict the possibilities for legend-making. If anything, these repetitions bespeak a stylistic attempt to redefine legend.[26]

Kerouac's legend, taking shape out of a desire to repeat events in the truth of the moment and thereby to revise by repetition, redefines the established idea of his work illustrated by Ann Charters's helpful but outdated linear notion:

The Legend of Duluoz begins with *Visions of Gerard*, his earliest years, continues into boyhood with *Doctor Sax* and adolescence with *Maggie Cassidy*, then goes on with *Vanity of Duluoz* into his college years and earliest encounters with Burroughs and Ginsberg. *On the Road* picks up when he met Cassady, mid-way into the writing of *The Town and the City*. *Visions of Cody* describes the cross-country trips and conversations with Cassady after Jack had discovered spontaneous prose. *Lonesome Traveler* and *The Subterraneans* describe his years working, traveling, and living in New York, filled with the frustration of being unable to sell any manuscripts after his first book. *Tristessa* describes the month in Mexico City before *The Dharma Bums*, while *Desolation Angels* continues after Berkeley to his summer as a fire-watcher and the publication over a year later of *On the Road*. *Big Sur* describes his alcoholic breakdown after

the assault of fame and *Satori in Paris* concludes with the loneliness of his final trip to Brittany.[27]

To counter this accepted notion of Kerouac's legend,
my study will posit a new grouping of core novels—a
new Kerouac canon—based upon the literary repetition
of the events of Kerouac's life in his attempt to elevate
the legend of his life to the level of myth. These canonical novels will be shown to constitute a stylistically "progressive" solution to the traditional Kerouacean problem.
The design will be immediately adumbrated in the chapter on *The Town and the City,* where Kerouac's first novel
is seen as the initial statement of Kerouac's preoccupations and values but in a style that he rejects in his later
novels and essays on writing. The following three chapters will show the successive *On the Road, Visions of Cody,*
and *Desolation Angels* as progressively solving the stylistic
problems encountered in the first novel. Moreover, each
of these novels solves the structural questions raised by
the one that precedes it. The end of the legend is the
completion of the circle of the Duluoz myth. The circular design, as chapter 6 shows, can also be seen in the
noncanonical novels, which repeat the central preoccupations exhibited in the core group, but which themselves become stylistic variations on the central themes
delineated in the chapters before. *Dr. Sax* and *Visions of
Gerard* demonstrate the Kerouacean notion of "Lost
Bliss," while *The Subterraneans* and *Tristessa* render "Bliss
Achieved." In the last chapter, *Big Sur* and *Vanity of Duluoz* form another grouping, the final Kerouac statement
of the themes that illustrate the unrelenting preoccupation of the legend at large—the ascension to the
sublime.

2

The Brothers Martin or the Decline of America

It is impossible to conceive a new philosophy until one creates a new language.

Norman Mailer
The White Negro

THE TOWN AND THE CITY is Kerouac's initial contribution to the Beat aesthetic stance. Even though the novel expresses the "beat" argument in more or less conventional terms, it can be seen as Kerouac's first experiment in form. A rather impressive first novel (not unusual for its autobiographical orientation), it serves as an apt beginning for the larger mythic opus, Kerouac's Legend of Duluoz. The novel also defines the ethos of the counterculture and gives the phrase "Beat Generation" a definition in depth, bringing to life an underground world Kerouac had come to know in New York in the late forties, peopled by a strange breed of American determined to pursue experience to its furthest reaches.

The conventional structure of *The Town and the City*—its overtly imitative aspect—simply does not define the true substance of the counterculture in question. At first, the novel seems to enact an archetypical American myth in a rather linear fashion: the cycle of the Martin family's ruin and collapse is the established form of the naturalistic genre of the American novel, one reminiscent of a Dreiserian "American tragedy" (though on Kerouac's more personal level of pathos). As in the case of *Huckleberry Finn*, what appears to be couched in rebellion is, in fact, part of the American tradition. Significantly, this tradition finds in Kerouac a linguistic solution to the problems it inherits.

The Town and the City is a coming-of-age novel and thus echoes the theme of many books of its day. Growing up as part of society at large, the coming into being of oneself—such issues are major obsessions of the postwar literary era. Yet this story can be told in any number of ways—the epic manner of Dostoyevsky's earlier family tragedy *The Brothers Karamazov* is but one striking example. Dostoyevsky portrayed this emergence of youth in the Freudian murder of the father, where each son represents an aspect of replacing parental values; taken together, the sons represent the ethos of a changing time.

Hermann Hesse has written of *The Brothers Karamazov* as a parable of "The Decline of Europe" in which he sees the author as the prophet of a loss of spiritual values.[1] Each son represents an aspect of the argument; each son defines a sensibility that is new and part of a prophetic vision: the physicality of Dmitri, the intellectuality of Ivan, the spirituality of Alyosha, the confusion of the bastard Smerdyakov. Each reveals a state of consciousness that questions and resolves the conflicts of the father. Thus the novel can be taken as a philosophical vehicle for the overthrow of an old structure represented by the father.

Kerouac was not unaware of Dostoyevsky and the nineteenth-century Russian novel in general, especially of its concern with the revelation of an emerging consciousness on the most primitive and psychological level of mythic intent. Kerouac says as much in a resonant passage of his *Book of Dreams:*

I had the Tolstoyan Dream, a great movie, with the . . . hero officer . . . the performance of the "Peasant"—the old Fellaheen hero—He is in Cossack soldier uniform, a soldier comes into his strange room to arrest him, the Peasant is just standing there,—with a sense that not only I but my father is watching this film, and it's in the 42nd Apollo and it's like the great lost Lost Father chapter of now—naturally out of print *Town and the City* and I remember my pre-tea joys, strengths and knowings God bless the purity of the Martins, the Kerouacs of my soul, still unfulfilled. (*BD,* 16–17)

An Everyman, a common worker or ordinary citizen up against an antagonistic society, becomes a recurrent figure in these dreams, just as an individual hero set against the American Dream shapes the myth of the entire Duluoz legend. The promise of America begins to look especially shabby in the instance of Kerouac's brothers Martin, as well as among the underground figures that Kerouac begins to represent in this early fiction.

The Town and the City is a philosophical and prophetic exposition of disappointment with the American Dream, using the family as the institution to represent the decline in values. The death of the father is a Dostoyevskian climactic point around which everything else pivots. But unlike the energetic senior Karamazov, George Mar tin dies the pathetic and passive death of an American tragic hero, and with him dies a sense of old-fashioned American values as well. The decline of the Martin family is described in direct proportion to the disappointments of the American Dream. As George writes to his wife:

"The poor American people! All the fools in the world take us for millionaires living in mansions. They attack us because we're supposed to have so much money and to be so arrogant because of it. . . . Some poor devil who works his heart out because his parents and grandparents had to work so hard and taught him the life of work too. And he is such a peaceable man, the American, the first really peaceable man!" (*TC*, 273)

Ironically enough, this is a statement of the American ideal of a good, principled American family that does everything right. But George dies poor, his business swallowed up by larger money concerns. This situation becomes the backdrop for the persistent justification for rebellion that permeates Kerouac's work as he continues to mourn this loss. The title of this first book could also be "The Old and the New," given the thematic treatment of the emerging psychological implications for Martin's sons as each one recognizes the banal realities that thwart the highest ideals of the simple, honest life.

The Anxiety of Wolfe's Influence

A history of the *The Town and the City*'s composition reveals how Kerouac's peculiar perception of American ideals becomes a revolutionary vehicle in both his ideology and style. The novel is, after all, a traditional novel. It resonates with the traditional literature and conventional strains of narration of the forties, has a linear overall structure, and has sentences that adhere completely to any handbook of English grammar. Begun in 1942, it took six years of work, most of it done at night, and was only finished when a cross-country trip in 1947 became a potent catalyst for completion. The book was begun just after Kerouac attended Columbia University in New York City and just before he met William Burroughs, Allen Ginsberg, and Neal Cassady. After this 1947 trip, Kerouac was all too eager to return to New York to complete his long overdue first novel and simultaneously began preliminary sketches for *On the Road,* "feeling that the form of the book he had been writing was too contained for the natural flow he wanted to release."[2] In other words, even in the final stage of writing this first novel, Kerouac was already thinking beyond the Wolfean style.

So just as on a thematic level the novel depicts the overthrow of the authority of the father, on a structural level the overthrow of a father—this time a literary one, Thomas Wolfe—may be seen as the book's secret literary drama.[3] Certainly the "natural flow" characteristic of Kerouac's later writings is not yet apparent in the linear syntax and development of *The Town and the City,* and so requires further clarification in this embryonic text.

In *The Town and the City,* Kerouac's particular "anxiety" is, of course, the influence of Wolfe.[4] In short, the kind of American prose tradition Kerouac follows most closely is the most sprawling, opaque, and impressionistic of the conventional modes. Above all else, Kerouac was a prose stylist, conscious in every way of what in Wolfe could potentially make for a remarkable new style. Indeed, the correspondences between these writers is evident in (1) their treatment of the effect of sensation: the child's delight in sheer sensation, the adolescent's romantic melancholy, the wild expectancy that flourishes in youth (Wolfe could write for hundreds of pages at a time about a vast sensory catalog of childhood experiences and reminiscences, exulting in landscapes, weather, awakening on a train late at night in some forgotten town, arriving in a foreign city); (2) their use of the theme of the gigantic American earth (the terrain evoked in Wolfe's novels is desolate, but its desolation is spiritual, like the devastating impermanence that haunts Eugene Gant and his brother Luke as they drive through small Southern towns); (3) their use of the nostalgic tone (Wolfe's sprawling style evokes a consistent nostalgia for a past which once held permanence as myth); (4) their reliance on the frantic mode of composition, (though Wolfe was well aware of the deficiencies of his sprawling style and admitted to his legendary editor Maxwell Perkins that *Of Time and the River* was flawed by his frenetic mode of working, which consisted in writing as fast as he could, for hours, days, weeks at a time, then assembling the result); and (5) their reliance on the dominance of the autobiographical impulse (Wolfe, before Kerouac, takes his place in the tradition of American writers who, like Whitman, create their fictions from the myth of themselves).[5]

Thus Wolfe opens Kerouac's eyes to America as a subject and theme in itself. Like the best of Wolfe's work, *The Town and the City* is a romanticization of social realism, a reworking of autobiographical material. But if the America of both Wolfe and Kerouac has a similar resonance of desolation, America also represents quite a different fatherland for each of them, and herein lies the critical point which neutralizes the notion of "imitation" as a condemnation of Kerouac. If anything, the new work must be seen as a perfection of the precursor.

Kerouac admitted his admiration for Wolfe and his instinctive response to model his writing on Hemingway, and Saroyan as well. But the novels of Thomas Wolfe especially affected Kerouac like "a torrent of American heaven and hell," as he put it, that "opened my eyes to America as a subject in itself."[6] Upon close scrutiny, this "torrent of American heaven and hell" evident in Wolfe has a great deal to do with Kerouac's own conception of the "natural flow," even before he was to achieve it in his own right. Both "torrent" and "flow" have similar definitions when applied to the writing process in Kerouac. Both imply ongoingness, energy, uncontrolled forces, but where "torrent" connotes danger, intensity taken to the extreme, "flow" connotes persistent openness. While effusion is the key, the force of such expressiveness underlines the differences between the two writers as much as their similarities and, for the purposes of this study, provides a methodology for understanding Kerouac's work as a whole.

The construction of the entire Duluoz legend is built on a series of repetitions, the repeated events of Kerouac's life. Each novel goes over material already expressed, restated at a different level of consciousness or perception, restructured again and again for greater personal as well as aesthetic clarity. Again Harold Bloom informs our notion of repetition for a more useful understanding of such a literary phenomenon. According to Bloom, "repetition never *happens*, but *breaks forth*, since it is 'recollected forwards.' "[7] Bloom goes on to suggest that repetition and recollection are in fact the same movement, only in opposite directions. This idea allows us a terminology and a technique for structuring Kerouac's thought according to a double movement that intertwines recollection and repetition and that unfolds at three levels: (1) what Kerouac calls the "torrent of heaven and hell" is the link to the past, the precursor, Thomas Wolfe; (2) Kerouac's "natural flow" is the present, that which must be released to arrive at the "truth" at the heart of his most basic precepts;[8] and (3) the "recollection forwards" is the movement of the writing into the future, the prefiguration of legend.

The thematic rebellion introduced in *The Town and the City* thus operates on a structural level because all three movements involve the breaking of order. Through repetition, ironically, all senses of time distinctions are overcome because the juxtaposition of past with present and then with future produces a sense of simultaneity. Time distinctions collapse. In addition, the very idea of repetition suggests how we can isolate the key or master rhetorical figures around which Kerouac's legend is structured. Rhetorical tropes—word groups, phrases, images, figures of style and thought—provide a matrix of signification structured in their repetition.

The New Language

The Town and the City represents the first stage in this evolution of Kerouac's language. The development of free prose will eventually become the solution to the linguistic problem that Kerouac encountered in the writing of his first novel and that led him to abandon *The Town and the City* in favor of the more experimental *On the Road*. That rebellion against the "father" is doubled at the level of Kerouac's literary paternity goes without saying.

Since free prose is influenced by jazz, the references in *The Town and the City* to the cultural milieu of jazz clubs is not merely historically significant. The novel contains not only overt mention of jazz clubs themselves but also a deliberate attempt to dissect and analyze the sources and patterns of the music itself, especially in the sections involving Liz and Buddy (the Martin sister and her husband, the jazzman). Kerouac's language had been enlarged by the phrasing he had heard in jazz clubs in the forties and fifties, just as Peter Martin's universe is enlarged by jazz in the final sections of the book. But with Liz and Buddy—and for Kerouac as well—there is also the more conscious concern with how chord progressions are used by a jazz singer or instrumentalist as a function of recollection, just as the alliterative tradition enabled the medieval practitioner of oral verse to perform this function. Here, though, it is the language of repetition in the Bloomian sense that is the organizing factor.

Buddy, for example, speaks of a particular Billie Holiday tune and associates it with the process of memory: " 'I just remembered a great song today!' cried Buddy. 'I'll bet you can't remember it. I'm going to make an arrangement of it. *She's Funny That Way!*' (*TC*, 222). What follows this explicit mention of jazz and the idea of composing or arranging is a rendition of the lyrics between sets of dashes that prefigure the writing Kerouac considers his most authentic. But while the ideology of this mode is set up in this early novel, it will be fully utilized only later, as part of Kerouac's solution on a structural level to problems here introduced at the level of theme: " *'I can't save a dollar—ain't worth a cent—but she'd never holler—she'd live in a tent—I got a woman—crazy for me—she's funny that way.* Think of the beautiful chord progressions in that, beautiful but simple, just pure!' " (*TC*, 222). This concept governs Kerouac's expressed philosophy about language—that is, be beautiful and true, but most of all true. The break-up of language signifies precisely such truth of emotion, impassioned perhaps, but in any case part of the drama of the rendition.

Following this mention of the Billie Holiday tune it appears that Kerouac's writing is influenced, either consciously or unconsciously, by the words he puts in Buddy's mouth, as in the sentimental tone of the following description: "Then they were almost asleep from the drowsiness of lapping water and the breeze, and the cool enfolding flower-smells all around, and the grass underneath them that was like warm hay in the cool night—the young lovers, on the starry shore at night, in the bower, dreaming of trains and far-off cities of jazz" (*TC*, 223). We can think of each phrase as a particular chord: the sentence is built upon two "and" clauses, the subject redefined in apposition to the subject "they," followed by two prepositional phrases and a verbal phrase indicating continued action, all in a progression. This is the beginning of Kerouac's sketching technique, which delivers units of thought from the typical English sentence patterns through a musical rather than traditionally literary idiom (James Joyce discounted, of course), as rebellion becomes structural and stylistic as well.

While the musical analogy dominates the later aspects of the legend more pointedly, the language of *The Town and the City* also doubles its thematic of rebellion at the level of the breaking of structures and forms. Thus characters run away from home, much as Kerouac attempts to do so at the level of style. For example, Joe Martin contemplates his life: " 'I'd like to know what I'm doing driving this truck. Just look out there: a highway, lights, a big moon above, a breeze blowing over the fields. Hear the music from that diner? See these cars going by with beautiful women? Back and forth, back and forth, from Boston to here, and what do we get for it?' " (*TC*, 91). Joe's question signifies the larger quest of Kerouac's fiction—the highway, lights, and moon are prominent images that are repeated not only in *The Town and the City*, but throughout the entire legend. The back and forth motion of Joe's thoughts prefigures the cross-country trips of Dean Moriarty and Sal Paradise, the characters of the next legend novel who exemplify similar types of rule-breaking and debunking of authority. Like Sal at the outset of *On the Road*, Joe suggests the collapse of the American ideal. He has three wives, though he has never been divorced. His question of why he drives the truck becomes the object of a philosophical quest. In fact, each brother in turn becomes a questing figure, looking for meaning and identity as the world around him seems to defy the ideal of American freedom.

Each brother struggles to free himself from a life-style associated with authority and responsibility (with father, god, and so on). Each Martin represents a variation on the theme of the overthrow of the authority of the father George, the prime exemplar of authority in the family structure. Each child must break with the family in order to come into his own being. And the action of each character therefore becomes a graphic progression away from the values of the past, which are both sentimental and seductive for each son. Each must undergo the pain of loss as each enters the realms of greater, more experienced consciousness, represented graphically by the eventual move to the city. But this action merely signifies on a psychological level the change in consciousness that all home-leaving (all expulsion from the garden) implies, and Kerouac undertakes this theme again in the novels *Maggie Cassidy* and *Vanity of Duluoz* with more or less the same resolution: that any drastic change of sensibility is an act of rebellion that is at once a necessity for survival and a wish for death. In some ways, a failure of *The Town and the City* is the insistence of this theme and the predictability of each son's experience as a result. In other ways, the manner by which each son figures into the polemical and philosophical design of the novel is artful for a first novel with so grandiose a scope.

Joe Martin, then, drives his truck as a vehicle of flight, its back and forth movement providing a jarring effect much as the wresting free from patterns of authority and control exemplified in the activity of hitchhiking also contributes to a restless movement within the narrative. Breaking free is further associated with a kind of lawlessness. For example, Joe's escapade with his buddy Paul ends up as a total act of childish impotence: "And thus, in this manner, without a second's forethought, Joe and his melancholy wild friend began a mad voyage that was to take them a thousand miles up and down the seaboard and into the middle west, in a truck which was now technically a stolen truck" (*TC*, 94). The narration is achieved in one sentence, hanging on clauses separated by commas. As this long prose line develops over the course of Kerouac's career, it acquires a musical lyricism by which Kerouac's best prose comes into its own. It eventually achieves a flow, whereas in this early part of his career, the writing is choppy, its references to flight—to voyages, the sea, time, geographic locations—are vague and dislocating.

The desire for flight from responsiblility is even extended to the family at the dinner table, the ultimate symbol of authority in the home. The dialogue that ensues is, however, still conventional, unlike the dialogue in Kerouac's later work. Joe talks excitedly about leaving: " 'I just feel like I'm hanging around doing nothing. You know it's terrific country out Pennsylvania, Ohio, out that way!' Joe cried eagerly. 'Out West, Pa!—I'd like to tear right out to California and see what kind of work they got there!' " (*TC*, 95–96). His excitement is infectious, and all the Martin boys want to join him. The mother finally asks what he will do for money and where he is going to stay. He replies, " 'I'm gonna hit the road, Ma! I don't need any money!' " (*TC*, 96). The *exclamatio* of this dialogue prefigures the excited speech to be encountered in later legend. Here, however, the speech indicates the restless attitude and impatience of the Martin boys as they grow up, mirroring almost exactly the state of Kerouac's developing style. To punctuate his flight, Joe's leavetaking comes surrepticiously: "The next day he told his mother he was going to a movie—so she would not feel bad—and he started out for California hitchhiking, just like that" (*TC*, 98).

Mickey's flight is parallel to his brother's, highlighted in his case by the rhetorical tropes of horse racing. As he and his father discuss the races, his speech makes a connection with writing, just as Buddy's speech has already made the connection between jazz phrasing and memory. Mickey says, " 'I'm gonna handicap them and write it on the typewriter' " (*TC*, 102). Then follows a characteristic Kerouacean preoccupation—that the most prominent place to study the true speech of America is the cafeteria:

So they talked about these things, and ate breakfast down at the Square in the cafeteria where the sun streamed in upon the clean tiled floor that had just been mopped, and everything was brown and gold—strong coffee brewing in the big urns, the fat half-grapefruits in the chipped ice all golden in the sunlight, the brown mahogany panels, the gleaming food counter, and all the men that were there in the morning eating and talking. (*TC*, 102)

The pacing here is similar to that of a horse race. This punctuation of repeated dashes forces the eye to read the clauses as quickly as possible in one catalog of images. This pacing exemplifies the beginning of Kerouac's mature, panoramic vision, which in one sweep will acquire the ability to heap detail upon detail so that the entire picture is seen at once, not piecemeal. This concern for the panoramic vision is an important aspect of the sketching technique, especially as it is used later in *Visions of Cody*. Still, the dashes and the inordinate number of clauses make for an interesting variation on the traditional English sentence as language becomes one form of authority against which Kerouac himself rebels.

Ironically—and to complete these figures of escape—the winning racehorse is known as Flight: " 'Flight! Flight! Look at her go!' yelled Mickey. With gloating disbelief they watched the russet-colored horse streak down the backstretch a full seven lengths in front of the pack and going away all the time, going away to ten lengths, running alone far ahead of the pack as though it were running for fear and faster all the time" (*TC*, 104–5). In this passage, the use of the present participle elongates the action, which accelerates with each clause and repetition. The syntax of description simply underscores the thematic element of escape.

Yet another aspect of this evolution of language is characterization. Each brother embodies a certain philosophical outlook on freedom and each in turn argues the theme of the overthrow of authority. Kerouac's procedure matches thematic and stylistic projects as the characters enact the attempt to overthrow fathers at the level of theme, while the language attempts to overthrow the "father" of literary influence.

Outside the Martin family, characters tend to function merely as catalysts for revolt. Examples include Joe's sidekick Paul (already discussed), and Francis's eccentric, politically inclined friend Wilfred Engels (not an accidental name), who instigates a change in Francis through their conversations. The account of their first meeting is telling: "What was most important to Francis was that for the first time in his life he heard spoken—and spoken in the articulate fluent language of 'contemporary thought'—all the misty indistinct feelings that he had been carrying around with him for the last few years in Galloway" (*TC*, 115). These characters, these catalysts of change, are of special significance because they prefigure Dean Moriarty's role in *On the Road*. Characters like

Will Dennison and Leon Levinsky are, like Dean, drawn from the characters in Kerouac's life who initiate change there as well—Dennison, for example, being based on William S. Burroughs and Levinsky on Allen Ginsberg.[9] Inevitably, then, these characters change the persona most aligned with Kerouac's own sensibility in *The Town and the City*, Peter Martin.

Moreover, language itself becomes a means of leaving the "town" figuratively, almost even literally. As a vehicle of escape in its own right, the language parallels the mechanisms of flight by reflecting a revolt in sensibility at large. Language change becomes the means of emerging in the "city." Through his friend Engels, Francis at last realizes that "other men and women wandered lonely in the world carrying in their hand the bitter proud fruit of 'modern consciousness. . . .' He [Francis] was amazed to think that a whole coherent language had sprung into being around this restless, intelligent, determined trend, this gentle, invisible revolt in America" (*TC*, 115). This speech ties the theme of the overthrow of authority witnessed in each son to the overall revolt in consciousness and style. The revolt on the thematic plane anticipates the linguistic revolt which will become further pronounced in the novels of later legend; the change in language patterns are beginning to be felt by Francis in the surface plot, and it is this change that initiates his revolt against the father.

Leaving Town as American Myth

If fathers are to be overthrown, then the myth of America is also both attacked and reconstructed in Kerouac's legend. The myth of America is Kerouac's vision of the ultimate Paradise or original home, in every sense as profound, spiritual, and unattainable as the Biblical one, and one exposed by the emerging consciousness of the movement from the "town" to the "city." But if the myth is criticized, it is also reconstructed by the change in sensibility, thus providing a double movement. A systematic mock-heroic design in *The Town and the City* runs counter to the design of breaking everything down. The image of restless, rebellious youth is heroic and mock-heroic at once, bringing the design of the novel closer to epic even as it tends to break the order we associate with epic proper.

In each brother there begins to be a concern for new values to replace the old ones, but within the shape of the novel only glimmers of such progression are evident. The novel repeats at the level of structure the design of the double movement we have already seen by juxtaposing a system of conventional heroic tropes with a concomitant system of tropes portraying a questioning, despairing sensibility; at the same time, in traditional mock-heroic manner, values are both exalted and debased by the heightening effects that aggrandize mundanities. The simultaneity of the heroic and mock-heroic dramatizes Kerouac's general ambivalence toward authority.

The first part of this movement can be seen in the repeated references to Jesus, Hamlet, and Homer. Peter Martin, for example, questions his existence as if he were Hamlet: "Who *was* he?" (*TC,* 126). But he enacts a peculiar kind of heroism, a contemplative and impotent kind, when he quits the football team in order to work in a printing firm to help the family, breaking his father's heart and disappointing the team as a result. He sees

himself as a star, with a nationalistic concern characteristic of the epic hero: "He was definitely 'hot'. . . . He
was going to become famous, he was going to be the
dark swift figure with twinkling feet that is seen in the
Pathé Newsreels galloping across chalk-stripes in the terrific, mob-swarmed, Autumn-dark stadiums of America
as jubilance strides across the land" (*TC,* 131). The
hyphenated adjectives are reminiscent of Homeric epithets, but in Kerouac these allusions are satiric, undercut by the second part of this movement. As Peter
contemplates life, "he realized what a strange sad adventure life might get to be . . . really, strangely sad"
(*TC,* 127).

This technique produces a tone of pathos, represent-
ing loss. Peter's friend Alex Panos is described as a young
Greek who was known to exclaim "Rosy-fingered dawn!"
(*TC,* 213) with indescribable delight. But Peter reflects:
" 'This is the way it will eventually end.' And, mysteri-
ously, Alex walked away for the first time in their friendship with absent-minded sorrow. The gods that had
whispered in his ear were neither deceiving, nor playful.
It was the last time they ever saw each other" (*TC,* 300).
A tragic tone is thus produced which transcends epic
and mock-heroic alike and lends Kerouac's sensibility its
peculiar combination of buoyancy and despair.

Within the structuring of the plot, the brothers become more like failed or beaten-down heroes as the
decline of their family, symbolized by the father's loss
of his small printing business, creates confusion in each
about the values of America and the spiritual values they
inherit. Peter and Mickey go to church and see Jesus
"suffering and heroic . . . dear great sacrificial Jesus the
hero and the lamb. . . . [T]he mighty drama of life's

meaning was marching all around them, these were the 'soreheads' of the earth indifferently turning away from immortality and heroism, abysmal, empty, and una-mazed. That was not for Peter, not for Mickey. They had to be heroes or nothing" (*TC*, 121). By the second half of the novel, the action-packed descriptions of foot-ball, horse racing, Thanksgiving Dinner, the intimations of greatness which prevail in the first half, are domi-nated by the tragic pathos.

Yet the novel's tragic pathos is radiant, especially in the recurrent and opposed images of red brick and red neon which eventually signify Kerouac's attitude about America throughout the Duluoz legend. At this early stage, the red brick mills of Galloway are juxtaposed with "stammering, brutelike America" (*TC*, 116), the red brick a symbol of solidity, of structures, of honesty and simplicity, but slow to change, to take on "modern con-sciousness" (*TC*, 115). Red neon, on the other hand, "red neon upon the cobblestones" (*TC*, 119), provides a coun-terpoint of transient values that underscores the shabby illusion of the American Dream even as it prepares us for the alternative vision to come.

As the Martin family is compelled by restlessness, by wanderlust, and by necessity, out of their original home, the imagery remains consistent: "the darkness by grimy redbrick warehouses, the cheap hotel with its red neon, . . . all the things in America that people notice when they go journeying, which they look at with a sense of awful loneliness and dread" (*TC*, 232). In fact, when the Martins must move out of Galloway to Brooklyn, de-feated, the image is almost personified as "a great mournful structure of red brick, . . . with hundreds of dusty, dark windows, . . . One vast part of the red wall, windowless, displayed a huge advertisement, showing a man holding his head in despair" (*TC*, 343). Without the tinsel effect of neon, without the blinding glare of light on windows, the illusion of the dream is impossible, the despair pictured graphically upon the advertisement, unredeeming and unredeemable.

As we might expect, *The Town and the City*'s plot climaxes in the death of the father. Peter asks, "And what was it that had killed his father?" (*TC*, 477). The question is itself oblique in its tenses and inferences. The death is taken as a sign for the passive victimization of the small man, a philosophical argument about a decline in ideals. Peter's question in fact initiates the search for ideals which will become the dominant questing motif of the Duluoz legend. The father's values are merely replaced by the sons's questions; in *The Town and the City*, a language bespeaking the attitudes of the Martin boys is not yet articulated. This is the problem Kerouac seeks to resolve at the next stage of legend in *On the Road*. *The Town and the City* fails linguistically to contain the emotions leaking from its structures. As yet the overthrow of fathers—both thematic and literary—is incomplete.

3

The Road as Transition

The Open Road. The great home of the soul is the Open
Road. Not heaven, not paradise. Not 'above.' Not even 'within.'
The soul is neither 'above' nor 'within.' It is a wayfarer down
the Open Road.

D. H. Lawrence
"Whitman"

I F *THE TOWN AND THE CITY* establishes the essential proposition of the Duluoz legend—that is, the
loss of spiritual values prophesying the decline of America and its soul—then *On the Road* extends this idea in a
picaresque mode. The soul journeys along the open
highway of America, in search of permanence, of values
that will endure and not collapse. Indeed, as the design
of the Duluoz legend unfolds, the progression of Kerouac's career becomes one in which his own persona
retreats further and further away from the distractions
of this world to the inwardness of writing, "telling the
true story of the world in interior monolog," as he recommends to writers in his "Belief and Technique for
Modern Prose."[1]

Thus, within the context of the entire legend, *On the
Road* functions as a transition both stylistically and the-

matically. The road becomes a structural option based on temporal progression as well as a metaphor for the conventional quest myth. The novel takes the central idea of *The Town and the City*—disillusion with the American Dream—and develops it into a quest for new values; that quest, however, ends only in increased despair and desolation.

According to the pertinent biographical and critical data, sketches for Kerouac's second novel were written while Kerouac was still working on *The Town and the City*, during a period of hitchhiking west, as "Kerouac began to appreciate the potential of a novel that would capture the vitality of America."[2] Clearly he felt that the earlier novel could not do so, and the criticism that it was "imitative" made him all the more certain to supersede the structural limitations of the conventional *The Town and the City*. Ironically enough, Kerouac's structural solution in *On the Road* is amazingly conventional considering all the bravado about breaking tradition attributed to the book at its first appearance. After all, the quest tradition is the oldest convention of the novel itself.

On the Road follows upon *The Town and the City* as a development of one narrative strand, most predominantly Peter Martin's; and indeed, Kerouac's second novel dramatizes that strand in the outwardly-searching mode of the traditional quest romance. Through the creation of a superlinear motif, a quest of hyperbolic momentum and episodic frequency, Kerouac's fascination with high-speed cross-country excursions brings quest romance into a distinctly twentieth-century mode.

But *On the Road* requires clarification beyond its explanation as a variation of the quest motif. The essential myth of the novel is the search for something holy, some-

thing lasting, something that will allow the narrator, Sal
Paradise, the genuine tranquility of his "hearthside"
ideals. In the process of that quest, he must renounce
the material and follow after Dean Moriarty as his guide.
The quest is for something as ephemeral as the holy
grail or as the Zen denial of the concrete in favor of the
spirit or soul.

Dorothy Van Ghent finds this quest for the holy a
redeeming feature of all Beat literature. She sees the
Beat myth as following authentic archaic lines. Thus the
hero, the angel-headed hipster, comes of anonymous
parentage, "parents whom he denies in correct myth-
ological fashion. He has received a mysterious call—to
the road, . . . [to] the jazz dens. . . . The hero is differ-
entiated from the population by his angelic awareness. . . . His myth runs along these lines toward the
familiar end, some sort of transcendence."[3] Though Van
Ghent is correct in focusing upon the heroic quality of
the quest and in isolating the special quality of that Beat
hero the angel-headed hipster, this definition lacks analysis and as such is far too narrow to encompass the quest
myth that is *On the Road.*

To be specific, *On the Road* is an elegiac romance.
According to the most recent critical theories on the
quest romance tradition in Western literature, there are
three developmental stages to this genre; elegiac romance is but the latest and most keenly aligned with
modernism.[4] Old romance, that of Gawain and Parzival,
directs our attention exclusively to the task and character
of the knight, who must overcome weaknesses of his
own character in order to merit his noble station and
warrant the reputation of chivalric gallantry and valor.
Romance changes radically, however, in the hands of

Cervantes, where the entire story becomes ironic. In this second stage, the structure of traditional romance is revised so that the knight no longer holds the center of attention, but shares the stage with another figure, the squire. The story's fundamental irony results from the fact that we are never quite sure whose values we are meant to share, the knight's or the squire's, but we are still led to admire chivalric service, gallantry, and valor even as we are also led to doubt them. The third stage, elegiac romance proper, brings us back to Kerouac.

On the Road can be seen as an example of the evolution of quest romance as it turns elegiac. The knight and squire of old are retained in the personages of Dean and Sal. While the knight is obsessed by the goal of the quest, the squire does not share in the knight's preoccupation, but instead seems satisfied to look meekly on. If Dean is driven by the immediate gratification of kicks, of fast cars, women, and drugs, Sal—Kerouac's surrogate—is the observer who views Dean as a catalyst for the only action he knows: writing. In old romance the knight undergoes the pain of change brought on by the rigors of his quest; in the second stage of romance, the knight and squire together undergo development during the course of the quest. In elegiac romance, the knight does not change at all; like Dean, he does not mellow, he experiences no enlightenment, his character remains constant. Instead, the squire, like Sal, is the center of attention. It is his character that develops and it is his enlightenment we must try to understand.

Thus the genre of prose to which *On the Road* properly belongs is one in which the narrator regains his identity by revealing it to himself. He accomplishes this task of self-enlightenment by telling a story about a person who represents loss to him in some sense—a person, for example, ridden by misfortune, or full of daunted hope—but whom he still admires. Dean's relationship to Sal is thus clarified: he represents a loss to Sal, what Sal hopes to realize by admiring only those who burn out like incandescent roman candles: "The one thing that we yearn for in our living days, that makes us sigh and groan and undergo sweet nauseas of all kinds, is the remembrance of some lost bliss that was probably experienced in the womb and can only be reproduced (though we hate to admit it) in death" (OR, 124).

A Freudian interpretation of this passage would reveal Sal's attachment to Dean to be far more instinctual and beyond conscious control than would be suggested by the narrative itself.[5] At times the relationship between Sal and Dean is seen more appropriately as one between a son and lost father or between two brothers lost to one another. At first Sal says of Dean, "he reminded me of some long-lost brother (OR, 10).[6] In the final lines of the novel Sal sums up: "I think of Dean Moriarty, I even think of Old Dean Moriarty the father we never found, I think of Dean Moriarty" (OR, 310).

Sal observes his object lost through his hero, and the novel is shaped to direct our attention to the narrator's sense of this loss, which he transmutes and refines. And because the hero is somewhat bigger than life and to that degree distinguished from humanity, the hero is almost an abstraction which Sal creates through memory and fantasy. It does not matter, therefore, that Dean fails to reach or even embody the goals of his quest for lasting values. What matters instead is that Sal as narrator reaches the goal for which Dean is a catalyst—the understanding and freedom which comes of telling his tale, celebrating the fact that he is both alive and free. He tells the story to celebrate further that he has survived on terms authentically his own.

In *On the Road,* Kerouac advantageously shifts from one kind of romance to another, from family romance to elegiac romance, to dramatize more effectively the central philosophical preoccupation of *The Town and the City:* the question of who killed the father. Dean can be seen as a larger-than-life heroic embodiment of the renewal and survival that overcome the "anxiety of influence"—and specifically, the authority of the father—of the earlier novel. In *Visions of Cody,* the novel that parallels *On the Road* in legend time, Kerouac refines and transmutes the sense of loss in a totally different manner—into subtle, expansive meditations, into vast tropes on time, memory, and art. But in *On the Road* he opts for the elegiac romance form.

Spontaneous Bop Prosody

In the same way that *On the Road*'s overall structure of plot—the zigzagging across America in hyperbolic adventures and kicks—suggests a linearity that eventually renders the elegiac romance form superficial and almost comic, the novel's language starts to take on the unique style we associate with Kerouac. *Visions of Cody* and *Desolation Angels* are both more successful exemplars of the language that is beginning to take hold of the temporal progression of *On the Road,* here initiated by a dissatisfaction with the limitations of a linear structure the novel sets in place only to criticize; but the extraordinary quality of the language in *On the Road* distinguishes the novel's stylistic break with the limitations Kerouac perceived in his earlier effort. A discussion of Kerouac's language will reveal (1) how linearity or seeming temporal progression is broken down into smaller structures or phrases which can be analyzed as tropes of collapsing and building, and (2) how the texture of *On the Road* is controlled by a musical metaphor whose seeming onflow contains rhythms and cadences, interior sound systems, in the manner of prose poetry—though the full resources of Kerouac's spontaneous bop prosody have yet to be achieved.

During this "road" or transitional period, Kerouac was in fact evolving his philosophy of spontaneous composition, that spontaneous bop prosody which he wished to develop through each subsequent creation. Kerouac's philosophy is, moreover, one which involves a discovery of language through a new definition of structure. Each novel subsequent to *On the Road* is an attempt to redefine structure as it solves formal problems through the discovery of resourceful properties of language. Thus the quest for language becomes the solution to Kerouac's problem of form, with language itself becoming the object of the quest motif from Kerouac's own perspective. As he says in his essay "Essentials of Spontaneous Prose," "Modern bizarre structures . . . arise from language being dead, 'different' themes give illusion of 'new' life."[7]

Much has been made of the manuscript of *On the Road*, which provides evidence of Kerouac's linguistic experimentation. It has a scraggly, raw look, jagged and unrevised. Its mode of composition is famous. It was first written on a roll of paper and consisted entirely of one sentence, which uncoils over two hundred pages when finally paginated. Ann Charters refers to the manuscript as a "teletype."[8] John Clellon Holmes even recalls Kerouac in the process of writing—how the typewriter clattered without pause, how Kerouac unrolled the manuscript thirty feet beyond the machine, "a scroll three inches thick made up of one single-spaced, unbroken paragraph 120 feet long."[9] John Tytell's description is the most specific: Kerouac wrote on "sixteen-foot rolls of thin Japanese drawing paper that he found in the loft, taping them together to form one huge roll." Calling it a "marathon linguistic flow," Tytell goes on to describe Kerouac's handling of the 250-foot single paragraph, "as it unreeled from his memory of the various versions he had attempted during the past two years, but writing now with more natural freedom, somehow organically responding to the Zen notion of 'artless art.' "[10] This methodology goes far to explain Kerouac's purposeful "natural flow," or "struggle to sketch the flow that already exists intact in mind."[11]

This methodology, however, is not to be mistaken for the product. After Kerouac's six-year search for a publisher, Malcolm Cowley, Kerouac's editor at Viking Press, finally printed the book—edited, punctuated, and paginated.[12] Gerald Nicosia describes some of the specific revisions of *On the Road:* how it had been retyped on regular bond, how "the roll had been turned into a 450-page manuscript," and how the manuscript had been divided into its five "books," among other changes. Nicosia sums up Kerouac's attitude to the revision: "If the present *On the Road* were false from the point of view of art, it was the version truest to reality, and so he couldn't dismiss it out of hand. . . . [A]s he wrote to Holmes, *On the Road*—even as it now stood—was a good deal less false than *The Town and the City*."[13] When Tytell suggests that *On the Road* is less successful than *Visions of Cody* because the latter is unedited and therefore closer to Kerouac's ideals,[14] he misses the artistic import of the earlier book as a transitional phase. Rather, each novel solves the structural problem of unrevised prose through a rhetorical paradigm, based largely on an analogy with the idiom of jazz. And not only does the paradigm work for Kerouac's legend as a whole, but within the linguistic structures of each novel as well.

The specific textual components of *On the Road* are explained by the jazz reference. First, the musical analogy for temporal progression is made explicit as Kerouac's fundamental modus operandi. He describes his philosophy of composition, "Blow as deep as you want to blow," as if he were thinking of a writer as a horn-player. But then he ties this description of his methodology to a rationale for the peculiarities of his punctuation: "Method. No periods separating sentence-structures already arbitrarily riddled by false colons and timid usually needless commas—but the vigorous space dash separating rhetorical breathing (as jazz musician drawing breath between outblown phrases)."[15] The words and phrases that occur between dashes have the semblance of linguistic entities unaligned with the conventional subject-verb arrangement of English sentences.

A different notion of time exists in these linguistic configurations. The sentence traditionally functions by framing statements and ideas within a past-present-future arrangement. The sentence fixes time and does not allow the movement, flashes, and fluctuations of Kerouac's intent. Thus the musical analogy allows Kerouac to work out a notion of time distinct from the temporality of conventional writing, less prosaic and more poetic, less linear than the overall structure of the adventure he suggests, more temporally dislocated than the traditional quest formula. Phrases become poetic utterances, " 'measured pauses which are the essentials of our speech'—'divisions of the *sounds* we hear'—'time and how to note it down' (William Carlos Williams)." Thus Kerouac's prose has a measured breath, and timing is the key to purity of rendition. Kerouac describes the procedure as follows: "Time being of the essence in the purity of speech, sketching language is undisturbed flow from the mind of personal secret idea-words, *blowing* (as per jazz musician) on subject of image."[16]

This is the beginning of Kerouac's aesthetic solution to the time and space problem he had encountered in his first novel. *On the Road* is the attempt to solve that structural problem. Even though his solution also involves an attempt to follow a prescribed form such as the elegiac romance, the musical metaphor suggests a nonlinear ideal that will eventually explode the superlinear form of "blowing" in *On the Road*. Kerouac will perfect this form in sections of *Visions of Cody* and *Desolation Angels; On the Road* is therefore transitional, not yet exemplary of the form at its fullest.

A continued examination of Kerouac's essay "The Essentials of Spontaneous Prose" in tandem with a close reading of sections of the text of *On the Road* will provide concrete evidence of a compositional process analogous to the structures of jazz and of a repetition of these musical structures that provides a deeper pattern than the novel's linear surface narration might suggest.[17] It is useful to remember that jazz music almost always works as the repetition of a series of chord changes. Key to this music is the notion of repeated forms that become redefined and redeveloped through each rendition of the series. Moreover, timing is of course not only important for the phrasing of jazz notes but also integral to the very articulation of certain phrases, ideas, and structures.[18]

Kerouac's descriptions usually begin with the privileged image of the "jewel center," as he calls it in the essay on spontaneous writing.[19] A particularly instructive example occurs when Sal, Dean, and their friends leave Louisiana and "Old Bull Lee" to head further west. The passage begins with an interlude, or introductory phrase: "What is that feeling when you're driving away from people and they recede on the plain till you see their specks dispersing?—it's the too-huge world vaulting us, and it's good-by. But we lean forward to the next crazy venture beneath the skies" (*OR*, 156). Here Kerouac is only partially conscious of the meanings of words, conjured up primarily to incite the "semi-trance," the state "without consciousness" which he recommends for all writers in the essay under examination. Visually, he sets up an impressionistic canvas of forms breaking apart like atoms, but contained by the "world" and "skies," as though he were looking through a fish-eye lens.

After this first sentence, Kerouac reaches the key word or "jewel center" of this association as he is transported to the unconscious state which he aspires to achieve in the writing of spontaneous prose: "We wheeled through the sultry old light of Algiers, back on the ferry, back toward the mud-splashed, crabbed old ships across the river, back on Canal, and out; on a two-lane highway to Baton Rouge in purple darkness; swung west there, crossed the Mississippi at a place called Port Allen" (*OR*, 156). The repetition of "back" develops in a typical build-up so that the pacing of the unconscious exposition that follows gains momentum. This momentum is further triggered by the assonance and alliteration that move the line of Kerouac's free prose. The initial *w* and long *e* sounds lead into the slant rhymes of "ul," "ol," and "Al." The short *a* of "back" is echoed in "splashed" and "crabbed," all intended to emphasize the "wheeling" motion that he is describing. The use of prepositions—"on," "toward," "out"—reinforces "wheeling," so that a great deal of ground is covered in a compact motion.

Note the pacing in the "unconscious" exposition that follows: "Port Allen—where the river's all rain and roses in a misty pinpoint darkness and where we swung around a circular drive in yellow foglight and suddenly saw the great black body below a bridge and crossed eternity again" (*OR*, 156). First, the repetition of "Port Allen" creates force. Second, the poetic affects are tighter. The rolling *r*'s of "where," "river," "rain," "roses," are picked up by "darkness," with "where" again creating a circular motion. The word "swung" is repeated; "around" picks up the rolling *r* as does "circular drive," which actually states what the writing accomplishes at the levels of both sound and sense. A change in light from "sultry old" to "yellow fog" signals a change in geographic detail to give the journey its proper significance—enlightenment. In the next breath, Kerouac sums up the meaning of the trip as a whole as a panoramic vision not confined to the concrete geographical detail (the "Suddenly saw" reflects such awareness). And the alliteration of the *b*'s in "black body below a bridge" suggests something still mysterious as the passage comes full circle in crossing the Mississippi (and eternity) again.

The next part of the paragraph picks up after this minirelease or exhilaration with a new "jewel center," even stronger than the first, building up rhetorically to

"What is the Mississippi River?" from which the answer gushes forth:

A washed clod in the rainy night, a soft plopping from drooping Missouri banks, a dissolving, a riding of the tide down the eternal waterbed, a contribution to brown foams, a voyaging past endless vales and trees and levees, down along, down along, by Memphis, Greenville, Eudora, Vicksburg, Natchez, Port Allen, and Port Orleans and Port of the Deltas, by Potash, Venice, and the Night's Great Gulf, and out. (*OR*, 156)

Here again certain repetitions of sound and punctuation carry the pace as Kerouac's definition of the powerful river at once echoes and reveals his admiration for its spontaneous flow. The short *o* sound of "washed" and "clod" is repeated in the next phrase, with "soft," "plopping," "from," "drooping," "Missouri," and "dissolving" all echoing with subtle changes the movement described. Again concrete physical images in nature remind Kerouac of eternity, the "eternal waterbed" an image for the sought-after ideal—that which never changes—the final end of the search, at rest, in the grave. An earth image of "brown foams" then becomes a point of departure for all the port cities and towns here enumerated. Gerund phrases such as "voyaging," adjectives such as "endless," the repetition of "and" (and the long *e* in between) redramatize ongoing movement, while "down," "along," "by," and "out" carry this movement and its meaning toward the ultimate metaphor for the gaping womb/grave, "The Night's Great Gulf." In a similar manner, each passage or section comes full circle to a release in a metaphysical image, which explains in part the litanous, lyrical quality of a language that aspires to the state of "semi-trance."[20]

In yet another section, the focus is on Sal's narration of the Ghost of the Susquehanna, a story that reveals the same structural ingredients that prevail in the previously quoted passage. The "jewel center" starts off: "I thought all the wilderness of America was in the West till the Ghost of the Susquehanna showed me different" (*OR*, 105). All of the resonant language that follows, with its rhythms and cadences, is related to the central myth of "America." Moreover, the supernatural element of the ghost is significant because Kerouac's idea of revelation turns on how natural objects can conjure universal, eternal truths. The desired end of the natural flow of language is thus the same as the desired end of myth.

The buildup and repetitive sound patterns mark the now familiar circular motion: "No, there is a wilderness in the East; it's the same wilderness Ben Franklin plodded in the oxcart days when he was postmaster, the same as it was when George Washington was a wild-buck Indian-fighter, when Daniel Boone told stories by Pennsylvania lamps and promised to find the Gap, when Bradford built his road and men whooped her up in log cabins" (*OR*, 105). Starting with the contradiction "No," emphatic in its signal to set off a new riff, the passage builds on a pioneering image that sees the great men of American history as common people (an idea repeated in Kerouac's image of America in *The Book of Dreams*). The notion is both Christian and democratic in its vision of each man's place under God and law. The *o* sounds of "no," "plodded," "ox," and "post" propel Kerouac's language, while the "when" functions to trigger a phrase as "back" does in the previously cited passage. Kerouac's unusual diction—the use of compounds such as "wild-buck" and "Indian-fighter"—and his use of onomatopoetic verbs like "whooped" attempt to create a literary language that echoes the language of America.

Central also—and paradigmatic of our other motif—is the emphasis on the idea of "building" and "collapsing." Optimism is expressed in the terseness of the adjectives and the idea of "promise." But this optimism is, of course, followed immediately by the down side of the vision, so that the description is actually controlled by a sense of opposition and contradiction: "There were not great Arizona spaces for the little man, just the bushy wilderness of eastern Pennsylvania, Maryland and Virginia, the backroads, the black-tar roads that curve among the mournful rivers like Susquehanna, Monongahela, Old Potomac and Monocracy" (*OR*, 105). This image therefore collapses the optimism of the previous sentence, showing the up-and-down movement of Kerouac's myth about America. The rhythmic and patterned sounds are created to present the optimistic and exuberant but also the sad and mournful. The idea of the "little man" conjures Kerouac's association with his father as he begins to understand the side of the American Dream that is destructive. Here "backroads" and "black-tar" emphasize the sorrowful aspect of the "promise" in the first part. Unlike the "great black body" that was a symbol of eternity earlier, these rivers seem sadly dead and, like conventional sentences, end-stopped.

But the next paragraph, predictably enough, must begin with a new jewel center: "That night in Harrisburg I had to sleep in the railroad station on a bench; at dawn the station masters threw me out" (*OR*, 105). Here Kerouac continues his narrative with a hobo image of himself, humbled by his "station." The dawn womb of the

station connotes expulsion, leaving the narrator to ex-
trapolate philosophically: "Isn't it true that you start your
life a sweet child believing in everything under your
father's roof? Then comes the day of the Laodiceans,
when you know that you are wretched and miserable
and poor and blind and naked, and with the visage of
a gruesome grieving ghost you go shuddering through
nightmare life" (OR, 105). This is a thematically and
structurally important passage, one that sums up much
of Kerouac's deepest paranoia about life, and one to
which all the narrative circles eventually point as they
oscillate between building and collapsing. This is the
vision of the innocence from which we start our childhood beliefs, a womblike paradise that becomes revealed
through the process of living. Part of Kerouac's litany is
a fond reminiscence of this state and the nostalgic sense
of loss that accompanies his life. But another part is a
sense that dream and reality partake of the same substance. This image of expulsion from paradise leaves
Kerouac likening himself (and all of us humble humans
as well) to a ghost, not in death but in life. The sense of
the dream or of paradise collapsing is thus all too real,
whereas the future afterlife is as yet unknown and an
end of the quest itself. The sounds build an image of
all-inclusiveness to this paranoia of possibilities: "ands"
link the adjectives "wretched," "miserable," "poor,"
"blind," and "naked," telling us that we are hallucinatory
images, each with the same abject visage—that of the
alliterative "gruesome grieving ghost"—which comes
from the collapse of the protective structure, the father's
roof.

A buildup of images of despair recounts Sal's hunger,
until a final apocalyptic image concludes part 1 as we

reach its consummate jewel center: "Suddenly I found myself on Times Square."

> I had traveled eight thousand miles around the American continent and I was back on Times Square; and right in the middle of a rush hour, too, seeing with my innocent road-eyes the absolute madness and fantastic hoorair of New York with its millions and millions hustling forever for a buck among themselves, the mad dream—grabbing, taking, giving, sighing, dying, just so they can be buried in those awful cemetary cities beyond Long Island City. (*OR*, 106)

The passage brings the journey full circle, literally and figuratively. Kerouac speaks of being "back" in Times Square, in a womblike image of America as a body. The sounds reinforce this notion: key words like "millions" are repeated, key syllables such as "ing" elongate action, the short *u* in "hustling," "buck," "among"—all these elements emphasize the circular return enacted thematically. The staccato rhythm of "forever for" moves toward the trope of the "mad dream" at the passage's center, a comment on the American Dream that becomes the key thematic element of the novel, and that finally ends in the grave, "buried" in "cemetary cities."

This passage goes on to conclude part 1 of *On the Road*. What is most evident in it is the rhythmic pulse that is taking shape in the writing, a pulse that arises from Kerouac's use of tropes that are original and yet follow a system that can be analyzed and determined. As Kerouac's story progresses, this language—especially in its ability to hold in a sustained tension both optimism and pessimism, up and down—becomes indistinguishable from the myth that it conveys.

"Everything is Collapsing"

On the Road achieves a rhetorical solution to the philosophical problem Kerouac faced in *The Town and the City*. The quest myth, in its linear, temporal progression seems adequate for the revelation of adventure. It relies, however, upon the conventional Christian tautologies that become insupportable as modernist notions interrupt the assumptions of absolutes and authority, of God, government, and of the Good. Kerouac's very questioning of these assumptions parallels a fundamental collapse of faith within society at large, which makes Kerouac's redefinition of the quest motif a reexamination of values at every point. Indeed, the language and myth of *On the Road* reflect an emotive as well as an aesthetic problem.

Integral to the mythic notion of the quest is the idea of the hero. Here he is identified at the outset: "I first met Dean not long after my wife and I split up" (*OR*, 3). This sentence appears banal enough, but not so after a reconsideration of *On the Road* as a system of tropes of collapse and rebirth. Since the narrative begins with an image of collapse and in its larger schema works out a circular pattern of building and collapsing again, the heroic action is unrelated to event and deed. In *Tom Jones*, by contrast, the picaresque quest motif frames action that is episodic and moves through climactic moments of plot. The dramatic Inn at Upton scene is a climactic turning point. Nowhere in *On the Road*, however, do we get a sense of one incident or another becoming more or less dramatic or illuminating to either the reader or narrator. Similarly, the contrast is exemplified in the creation of the hero, who in the eighteenth-century novel acquires that identity in the process of the quest. In *On the Road,* Kerouac extends the characterization described in *The Town and the City* by ascribing a mock-heroic heightening and diminishing to characters to underscore the up-and-down movement at large. Sal relates the adventures of his friends, especially Dean ("the Holy Goof"), calling them clowns and angels at once. Hence the heroic heightening in *On the Road* stems from the hyperbolic mood, is ironic, and is derived from the bold assertions of heroism Sal attaches to the comedic gestures of his friends, likening those angels to Groucho Marx and W. C. Fields. We are moved through a series of heightened moments of "meaning-excitement"[21]—each being part "up," part "down," as the linguistic experimentation requires them to be—that Kerouac himself terms moments of "IT." "IT" is both integral to the notion of the hero and to the quest. The cyclical movement of tropes becomes "riffs" that culminate in "IT." "IT"—as I shall show—is thus the real object of the quest.

Because "IT" is an isolated moment, it is necessarily defined by a solid structure against which "IT" can be contrasted. "IT" is like a chord progression off Kerouac's central red line (Route 6) across America; for Kerouac the country is physical, solid, like a body or "the great raw bulge and bulk of my American continent" (*OR,* 79). This solid structure indicates that the long red line that leads from the tip of Cape Cod clear to Ely, Nevada, and on to Los Angeles is a significant system of signposts, symbolic of something concrete and whole, which might also signify some direction. But, says

Sal, "It was my dream that screwed up, the stupid hearthside idea that it would be wonderful to follow one great red line across America instead of trying various roads and routes" (*OR*, 13). Sal's sense of direction is thrown off most by Dean. Sal laments, "With frantic Dean I was rushing through the world without a chance to see it" (*OR*, 205). As we might expect, tropes of collapsing are juxtaposed with tropes of concrete images to strike the overall thematic chord, "Everything is collapsing" (*OR*, 56, 99). Likewise moments of "IT" shatter the continuity of the cross-country excursions, like variations off the central theme, with each exposition quite technically a riff.

The analogy of "IT" with the action of the jazzman is made explicit in the text. The alto player is described: "He starts the first chorus, then lines up his ideas. . . . All of a sudden somewhere in the middle of the chorus he *gets it*—everybody looks up and knows; they listen; he picks it up and carries. Time stops" (*OR*, 206). This description proclaims the terms of Kerouac's aesthetic stance as much as his more explicit statements in the essays and *Paris Review* interview. He indicates the purposes of establishing such an aesthetic as an effective mediation of time and space. At the moment of "IT," time stops. But as the description goes on, Kerouac describes a movement in space: "He's filling empty space with the substance of our lives, confessions of his bellybottom strain, remembrance of ideas, rehashes of old blowing. He has to blow across bridges and come back to do it with such infinite feeling soul-exploratory for the tune of the moment that everybody knows it's not the tune that counts but IT" (*OR*, 206). In other words, it is not the continuity of causal relationship of experience that counts, but the heightened moment.

Kerouac enlarges on the meaning of "IT" by alluding to Wilhelm Reich, whose work Kerouac was reading during the period prior to the writing of *On the Road,* and who is specifically mentioned as yet another figure of "collapse." When Old Bull Lee suggests that the others try his orgone accumulator to "put some juice in your bones" (*OR,* 152), the explanation is that "according to Reich, orgones are vibratory atmospheric atoms of the life-principle. People get cancer because they run out of orgones" (*OR,* 152). Later, the mention of Reich at moments of "IT" are related to "complacent Reichian-alyzed ecstasy" (*OR,* 200). "IT" therefore represents some form of isolated and radiating pleasure as a feeling and end in itself, unallied to some purpose or spiritual accomplishment.

Rather than heroic action in conventional terms then, "IT" is satisfying as a form of instant gratification, a thrill for the moment, an epiphany. This momentary satisfaction becomes more significant to Sal than the pursuit of more conventional values such as permanence and ultimate security—the delusion of the hearth. Sal's attraction to Dean's amorality is thus explained, albeit fraught with ambiguity and concomitant irony:

I shambled after as I've been doing all my life after people who interest me, because the only people for me are the mad ones, the ones who are mad to live, mad to talk, mad to be saved, desirous of everything at the same time, the ones who never yawn or say a commonplace thing, but burn, burn, burn like fabulous yellow roman candles exploding like spiders across the stars and in the middle you see the blue centerlight pop and everybody goes, Awww! (*OR,* 8)

The heroic ideal is imaged through an ironic stance of madness, which has the ecstatic effect of Reichian energy but, as we might expect, at the same time the impermanence emphasized in the quality of "burn," three times repeated; "IT" represents the greatest high and the ultimate low simultaneously. The tenorman who has just achieved "IT" says, " 'Life's too sad to be ballin all the time . . .' " (*OR*, 199).

In order to create the effect of simultaneity of antithetical images, then, Kerouac uses intertwining rhetorical tropes of building/collapsing with the concomitant emotive response of ecstasy/sadness. In these antitheses/extremes, Kerouac depicts the spiritual decline of America. This decline becomes the object lost in the elegiac romance genre because these values and their loss are personified by Dean. Moreover, as these tropes develop in the narrative, a design takes the place of plot: the intertwining rhetorical tropes intersect at moments of "IT" in Kerouac's schema. Otherwise, they move through the narrative to a syncopated beat. Indeed, the musical metaphor allows Kerouac to solve the artistic problem not only of how to represent these antithetical images, but also how to build into them a double charge of affect. *On the Road* therefore becomes a paradigm for his state of vision both structurally and emotively. And thus the double signification of "beat" is realized as a thematic end in itself.

This simultaneous rendition of opposites solves the organizational problem of Kerouac's myth by centering itself on the double signification of "beat" in its antithetical meanings of both "down-and-out" and "beatific." This is the inference of "IT" on the mythic plane as well as on the structural level. Only in this pattern can the shifting ambiguities and complexities of unidealized existence become a parody of the American Dream romance through which Kerouac can take his ultimate ironic stance about America—that it is beat.

The plot of *On the Road* zigzags just as Kerouac's prose zigzags. The end of the linear road is death, but Kerouac has attempted to resolve the structural problem in a reassessment of linearity. The musical analogy and the redefinition of the quest form suggest a spatial, nonlinear relationship of language and form. *On the Road,* though, is only a temporary solution. The stylistic progression of the later novels makes this point evident. The structure of *On the Road* only suggests the desired effect of the simultaneity of antithetical images which is articulated at the next stage of legend in *Visions of Cody.* The road is merely transition.

4

Modalities of Consciousness

The reason why there are so many things
Is because the mind breaks it up . . .

Kerouac
"176th Chorus"

ALLEN GINSBERG EXPLAINS Kerouac's poetic sensibility:

It wasn't that Kerouac couldn't do the same thing with regular meaning prose; it was that he was suddenly aware of the sound of the language, and got swimming in the seas of sound and guided his intellect on sound, rather than on dictionary associations with the meanings of the sounds. In other words, another kind of intelligence—still conscious, still reasonable, but another kind of reason, a reason founded on sounds rather than a reason founded on conceptual associations. If you can use the word reason for that. Or a "modality of consciousness."[1]

The term "modality of consciousness" signifies the aesthetic recreation of the musical metaphor discovered in *On the Road,* only this time turned inward in *Visions of Cody.* Kerouac was not happy with *On the Road* as it appeared in its published form in 1957. Moreover, John Tytell claims that the novels written in the period of frustration between the actual completed manuscript of the original *On the Road* in 1952 and the edited version published in 1957 best exemplify Kerouac's talent and ingenuity in craft because they were not written with any promise of publication whatever. Most important, says Tytell,[2] is *Visions of Cody*, originally published in part in 1960 and then published posthumously in 1972 in its entirety—a cumulation of experiments in form, centering on the Kerouacean hero Dean Moriarty (Neal Cassady), now named Cody Pomeray.

Indeed, the material from the picaresque *On the Road* to the Proustian *Visions of Cody* reveals the development of Kerouac's craft from a linear narrative mode to a nonlinear one as he progresses toward the fulfillment of his writing ideals. A nonlinear form erupts from the linear *On the Road* because the material bursts out of the structure. In *Visions of Cody*, there is, by contrast, the renunciation of a linear prose in favor of a more sprawling, impressionistic writing that takes "free prose" to the outermost definition—prose still, but verging on poetry.[3] In each book thus far, Kerouac has solved a structural problem presented by the one before. With *Visions of Cody*, the conscious break with formal novelistic structure is an attempt to arrive at his sought-after "truth of the heart," unimpeded by conscious thought patterns.[4] The technique he evolves in this pursuit is meant to break through the subject/verb/object linearity of conventional prose forms. We should remember too, however, that though Kerouac brings the problems of his life to bear upon his books, this pursuit for the "truth of the heart" should be taken as a metaphor for the refinement of a technical methodology.

As the most experimental of all Kerouac's novels, *Visions of Cody* reveals multiple possibilities for novelistic expression. The five major sections demonstrate new aspects of Kerouac's style. The first two main sections are prose sequences wherein each statement does not necessarily rely upon what has come before for coherence, since Kerouac's coherence is not controlled here by chronological development. That the sequences are arranged in a more random order is suggested, for example, by the fact that several of the smaller sections that were printed under the title "Manhattan Sketches" in the anthology *The Moderns*[5] are not ordered as they were in the original text. This reordering suggests an interchangability of writing sequences that challenges narrative form, or at least that suggests a redefinition of novelistic coherence. These initial sections are followed by "The Frisco Tape," literally a transcribed tape of conversations between Jack (Duluoz) and Cody Pomeray that emphasizes the importance of natural as opposed to schooled or structured language. Following this section is an imitation of the tape in which Kerouac reinvents the basic ideas presented in the tape. These sections reveal the height of Kerouac's experiment in the search for a language that will adhere to his principles of writing: Kerouac's experiments involving the actual transcription of tapes and/or their imitation attempt to erase the "fiction" of narrative form entirely. Finally, "Joan Rawshanks in the Fog" is a revision of central Kerouacean preoccupations drawn through the filter of the ultimate "American scene," a Hollywood movie set featuring Joan Crawford, her name transposed by Kerouac's slant rhyme. In toto, these five sections suggest an enlarged conception of both novelistic structure and literary language that involves experimentation with nonlinear writing to achieve meaning in a circular fashion through a matrix of impressions.

Thus Kerouac's basic problem is to restructure time and space beyond what he was capable of creating in the limited linearity of *On the Road.* Understanding this change in the concept of expression is crucial to understanding the change in novelistic shape. While Kerouac wrote *On the Road* on an endless roll of paper in essentially one sitting that lasted two weeks, *Visions of Cody* was written in separate sittings, sections, and styles, in an attempt to grope for new language. In fact, *Visions of Cody* can be seen as a revised *On the Road,* if we take Kerouac's renunciation of revision as not precluding expansion, as Tytell does.[6] The change is fundamentally related to the shape of Kerouac's language.

Indeed, *Visions of Cody* is Kerouac's basic experiment with "free prose," a poetic kind of prose that Kerouac developed to render best the thematic material of *On the Road.* The frustration of his limitations in that novel made him keenly aware of a structural problem with his writing. As in *On the Road,* Kerouac is dealing with the creation of an aesthetic to incorporate antithetical mythic properties into a new work. In *On the Road* the solution was to allow such properties to exist simultaneously. But in a linear framework, the degree of his success is largely forestalled. In *Visions of Cody* he solves this aesthetic problem through "free prose," through language.

Hence *Visions of Cody* reads much like an interior *On the Road.*[7] Kerouac's use of "free prose," not only defines this narrative form but now introduces a new theme to the entire Duluoz legend as well—the evolving central preoccupation with the writer/self. The function of this writer/self as narrator is to develop his own perception through the sketching and spontaneous bop prosody Kerouac has already postulated but has not yet made into linguistic form. Thus the revelation of consciousness and language influence one another reciprocally.

In *Visions of Cody* the evolving language and consciousness of the writer/self finds a form consistent with the reflexive "I." This form is properly considered the "free prose" I have already discussed through the analogy between prose and music. Again, "free prose" is based on the irregular rhythmic cadence of the recurrence, with variations, of phrases, images, and syntactical patterns. In prose form Kerouac is thus enabled to collapse the thematic linear quest material of *On the Road* in favor of a circular design, "free" in terms of the writer's process but highly patterned by laws of its own integrity. The result of this style is the effect of simultaneity and the subsequent collapse of thematic oppositions in favor of a reigning ambivalence, both in the breakdown of the linear, the consecutive, the chronological—the cause-and-effect approach to recounting events—in favor of the illusion that everything (the entire cycle of birth and death, sense, perception, and so on) is happening at once and in the linguistic breakdown of clear, meaningful sentences in favor of recurrent phrases, images, and syntactical patterns that convey meaning by juxtaposition. This juxtaposition can be examined in terms of three registers that may be called in turn synaesthesia, synchronicity, and syncopation.

These registers or levels will go far to explain the recurrent rhetorical patterns of *Visions of Cody.* Synaesthesia, synchronicity, and syncopation are techniques that

Kerouac developed through his study of jazz music—his frequent trips to jazz clubs as recounted in the novels, his experience of reciting his writing with a jazz backup. But his understanding of the music is actually limited to what he could adapt to his prose. In *Visions of Cody* the techniques of experimentation all conspire to underscore Walter Pater's notion that "all art constantly aspires towards the condition of music," since in music alone the "constant effort of art" is to "obliterate" or interfuse the distinction between "matter" and "form" already realized by the medium itself.[8] Thus for Kerouac the musical analogy provides a model of coherence and unity where none of the traditional literary models will allow it. Time and space are so arranged as to repress or dismiss linearity and temporality as well. The zigzagging motion of *On the Road* is preempted by prose paragraphs of about a page in length, each a matrix of impressions of accumulated images, phrases, and syntactical patterns.

Synaesthesia, Synchronicity, Syncopation

Here is the technique in action. The section on Hector's Cafeteria in the first part of *Visions of Cody* (alternately printed as "Manhattan Sketches")[9] reveals Kerouac at the height of his craft:

I went to Hector's, the glorious cafeteria of Cody's first New York vision when he arrived in late 1946 all excited with his first wife; it made me sad to realize. A glittering counter—decorative walls—but nobody notices noble old ceiling of ancient decorated in fact almost baroque (Louis XV?) plaster now browned a smoky rich tan color—where chandeliers hung (obviously was old restaurant) now electric bulbs with metal casings or shades—But the general effect is of *shiny food* on counter—walls are therefore not too noticeable—sections of ceiling-length mirrors, and mirror pillars, give spacious strange feeling—brownwood panels with coathooks and sections of rose-tint walls decorated with images, engraved—But ah the counter! as brilliant as B-way outside! Great rows of it—one vast L-shaped counter—great rows of diced mint jellos in glasses; diced strawberry jellos gleaming red, jellos mixed with peaches and cherries, cherry jellos top't with whipcream, vanilla custards top't with cream; great strawberry shortcakes already sliced in twelve sections, illuminating the center of the L— Huge salads, cottage cheese, pineapple, plums, egg salad, prunes, everything—vast baked apples—tumbling dishes of grapes, pale green and brown—immense pans of cheesecake, of raspberry cream cake, of flaky rich Napoleons, of simple Boston cake, armies of éclairs, of enormously dark chocolate cake (gleaming scatological brown)—of deepdish strudel, of time and the river—of freshly baked powdered cookies—of glazed strawberry-banana desserts—wild glazed orange cakes—pyramiding glazed desserts made of raspberries, whipcream, lady fingers sticking up—vast sections reserved for the splendors of coffee cakes and Danish crullers— All interspersed with white bottles of rich mad milk— Then the bread bun mountain— Then the serious business, the wild steaming fragrant hot-plate counter— Roast lamb, roast loin of pork, roast sirloin of beef, baked breast of lamb, stuff'd pepper, boiled chicken, stuff'd spring chicken, things to make the poor penniless mouth water—big sections of meat fresh from ovens, and a great knife sitting alongside and the server who daintily lays out portions as thin as paper. The coffee counter, the urns, the cream jet, the steam— But most of all it's that shining glazed sweet counter—showering like heaven— an all-out promise of joy in the great city of kicks.

But I haven't even mentioned the best of all—the cold cuts and sandwich and salad counter—with pans of mountainous spreads of all kinds that have cream cheese coverings sprin-

kled with chives and other bright spices, the pink lovely looking lox—cold ham—Swiss cheese—the whole counter gleaming with icy joy which is salty and nourishing—cold fish,
herrings, onions—great loaves of rye bread sliced—so on—
spreads of all kinds, egg salads big enough for a giant decorated and sprigged on a pan—in great sensuous shapes—
salmon salads—(Poor Cody, in front of this in his scuffled-up
beat Denver shoes, his literary "imitation suit" he had wanted
to wear to be acceptable in New York cafeterias which he
thought would be brown and plain like Denver cafeterias, with
ordinary food). (*VC,* 10–11)

The overall effect of this passage is broken up by long
phrases set off by dashes, not by the long and short
pauses indicated by periods and commas in conventional
sentence patterns. Rather, Kerouac's method achieves
(1) the effect of the long breath (synchronicity), (2) the
effect of the intertwining tropes (syncopation), and (3)
the effect of the long bombardment of images (synaesthesia). These aesthetic effects together achieve the effect of simultaneity. The structure, furthermore, is not
random but reveals the tendency of Kerouac's writing
to radiate an all-inclusiveness. The repeated tropes reveal the latent patterns of the seeming "free prose" as
they repeat the preoccupations of Kerouac's mind; there
is method to the seeming randomness, which contradicts
the notion that Kerouac's nonlinear writing lacks
coherence.

The passage's interior design suggests it to have a set
of intrinsic structures that are a microcosm of the ex-
trinsic order of Kerouac's legend process. The structures
form a coherent set of linguistic oppositions that provide
the antithetical meanings that were so difficult for Kerouac to create in *On the Road.* Thematically, Kerouac is

thus enabled to signify the simultaneous antithetical movements of his story.

First, Kerouac gives the context: "I went to Hector's." Here a general statement locates the passage within the narrative and explains the significance of it for the Beats; Kerouac's description is meant to invest the place with special meaning and excitement, and, appropriate to the legend, give it special historical significance. The idea is then extended in the phrase, "the glorious cafeteria of Cody's first New York vision." The hyperbolic aspect of the writing overstates both the mock-heroic and the mundane reality of the simple experience of going to a New York cafeteria. A key theme thus emerges—"Everything is holy"—a theme introduced first in *On the Road* but here amplified and given breadth. The double signification of "beat" as both "down-and out" and "ecstatic" is given linguistic form. Because we see the ecstatic side, we know the sad will follow, or at least that it will abet the vision and thereby complete it.

Thus Cody, the central figure, is established as the quester, searching for values in the next phrase, "when he arrived late in 1946 all excited with his first wife." Cody's character is caricatured through a familiar trope, a comedic gesture or mannerism reminiscent of the Dostoyevskian holy idiot—in Kerouac's idiom, the "holy goof" of *On the Road*. The phrase "all excited" is meant particularly to recall Dean's initial description in the earlier book as one of the mad ones, totally excited by life, which so attracted Kerouac's Sal Paradise persona. We might well recall here the initial sentence of *On the Road* ("I first met Dean not long after my wife and I split up" *OR,* 3), which immediately associates Dean with disappointment about social restrictions at large. In this passage from *Visions of Cody*, however, the association is with excitement, its opposite. But when Kerouac also uses the word "late," this adverb foreshadows the disappointment which completes the excited picture. The image contains the multifacets of Cody's symbolic relation to the narrator in the novel, Jack Duluoz. Simultaneously, the character embodies opposite extremes within himself—the excitement which is the representation of hope, along with the lateness which anticipates the Duluoz disappointment in his hero. Even if we take the "late" as it is meant in the phrase "in late 1946," the force of setting the time in such a way bodes disappointment because the prepositional phrase, "with his first wife," is meant to expand upon the previous impression, with an ironic reference to societal values. In the late forties, divorce was un-American and therefore unthinkable, except to renegades like Cody/Dean. Implicit in the line is the idea of divorce as another rift or breakup of values, implicit because "first" implies "second."

The general context that opens this block of Kerouacean writing next reveals the narrator's (writer/self's) feeling about what he is about to describe: "it made me sad to realize." This phrase indicates another movement in the writing, from general to particular and then to the generalization within the particular. Hector's Cafeteria becomes the "jewel center" from which the rest flows in a panoramic vision that tends to generalize the detail but also eclipses the movement through sounds and image to the "heart" of his meaning—the natural innocence Duluoz finds in his subject's vision, a fresh view of a scene that will, however, be revealed as complicated and all-inclusive even though there is a slick veneer.

Kerouac proceeds with the description of the cafeteria counter as if it were a banquet at the Palace of Versailles. But the glorious, over-aggrandized language of color and sensuous detail is undercut by disappointment. Each image radiates meaning by stating one thing and also suggesting its opposite. Simultaneity is thus created as the beatific and beat are instantaneously contained in a single (really double) movement. For example, the detail in the "glittering counter" exemplifies this movement. Set up as a seemingly endless image, the counter has a sprawling quality, emphasized by the present participle. Furthermore, the idea of glittering really seems to have little to do with this subject and environment, except by ironic contrast. This descriptive technique is Kerouac's form of synaesthesia, the technique of transferred sensation, where sensation is produced at a point different from the point of stimulation; the subjective response normally associated with one sense is in fact stimulated by another sense, as in hearing color in a certain sound. "Glittering" as a visual image is here meant to evoke perfection, much as a Christian image like the Holy Grail signifies perfection. But it simultaneously signifies the opposite, the ironic and material tinsel effect. Following the dash, the phrase "decorative walls" sets limits to the seemingly endless quality of the counter, the boundaries within the descriptive term "decorative" implying unnaturalness and foreshadowing the opposition of the image that precedes it. After dashes, another antithesis is emphasized in the repetition of n sounds—the feeling of decadence is almost baroque. Old is contrasted with new, but with the understanding that old is more "noble" as "nobody notices," while the ceiling has now browned into a "smoky rich tan color." After this contrast, Ker-

ouac situates images of light in this same juxtaposition—
"chandeliers" replaced by "electric bulbs within metal
casings or shades"—as if to indicate that the true light
is at least partially hidden. In keeping with Kerouac's
overall design, the sense of nostalgia signifies that old is
better.

Next, Kerouac retreats from the meticulous detail to
a reiteration of the "general effect" of the counter, introduced by a "But" and with "shiny food" underscored.
Some of the following detail will therefore involve antithesis too, concentrated on the general effect of shininess. Shininess is not only radiating, original light, but
also reflected light; moreover, it has the sense of excel-
ling or being conspicuous in splendor, beauty, or brilli-
ance. Light is apparently useful to Kerouac as a way of
making everything look holy. He even goes on to elaborate on the effects of light: "walls are therefore not too
noticeable," which suggests that the blinding effect of
shiny light gives the illusion of breaking walls or limits
down. In the next phrase "sections of ceiling-length mirrors, and mirror pillars, give spacious strange feeling."
This phrase produces the simultaneous effect of reflection back and forth so as to render a limitless feeling of
expansion. So all-inclusive in the image-mechanism of
expansion lies its flip-side as well—limitation.

Mirrors, of course, give a false, inverted image, which
can be illusionary. A contrast between the material objects of this world and the truth of the writer's heart is
therefore emphasized. The failure of the images to render the description of anything more than the material
world suggests that the writer can only hint at a tran-
scendent quality that is merely suggested by the gleaming, shiny, and tinsel-coated. This quality is even

underscored by a playful sound system: the paralleled assonance of mirror/pillar and the preponderance of sibilants. The illustration continues as Kerouac emphasizes the wood-panel detail "decorated with images, engraved," a hint of religious iconography. But the decoration is also unnatural, emphasized in turn by "rosetint walls," an image which belies a notion of falsity, the false image of mirrors. A major theme of the Duluoz legend is thus introduced, a theme that contrasts reality with appearance, with the added Christian notion that nothing in this world is what it seems; that no matter how attractive the appearance of some worldly objects, they are nothing in comparison to the attractiveness of the spiritual. Nothing secular approaches perfection.

The following section begins in *exclamatio,* Kerouac's celebrated exuberance. Like the refrain of a song, Kerouac repeats the image of the counter, with the added "ah" of pleasure. He emphasizes the brightness of neon light "as brilliant as B-way outside." This ordinary image of a cafeteria counter has taken on the hyperbolic aura of an aggrandized description that builds to the heightened crescendo of "great rows of it." "IT," the moment of heightened reality.

"IT" is now the "jewel center" upon which Kerouac will expound, and which now transports him to his semitrance in order to make his word hoard flow. "One vast L-shaped counter" indicates his interest in shape, as much as "vast" indicates his interest in expansiveness; both concerns introduce the synaesthetic passage that follows: ". . . great rows of diced mint jellos in glasses; diced strawberry jellos gleaming red, jellos mixed with peaches and cherries, cherry jellos top't with whipcream, vanilla custards top't with cream. . . ." Notable are Kerouac's visual and sound systems, hardly random as we might first expect, but organized in Kerouac's schema of antithetical imagery. First, he explains the general impression suggested by the expository section just described; he moves into the particular in a torrent of vivid color and textual images that provides contrasting oppositions: the "diced" repetition alludes to a virtually cubist effect he hopes to achieve, hard edges juxtaposed with one another. The diced forms reveal the oppositions hard/soft in translucent images—the fruit suggests Eden-like primitiveness in nature, as opposed to civilization's neon. Second, in sound there is an interlocking phrase system; pauses and glides provide syncopation in the repetition of "jello," "top't" (the elision indicates a conscious and deliberate effort toward the rendering of syncopated sound), and "cream." This sound system is an example of "free prose" at its best.

This flow of language is followed by "great strawberry shortcakes already sliced in twelve sections, illuminating the center of the L. . . ." The repetition of "great" underscores the aggrandizing images and links the phrase to the preceding one, completing the repetitions of sibilant sounds and the assonance of contrasting long and short vowels. These sound patterns emphasize the attention to light, exalted as in an illuminated manuscript or spiritual text, or simply the shedding of light and an increased awareness and understanding. The image of a cake cut in slices, furthermore, is reminiscent of a mandala, a holy circle of miniscule detail which this description mimics.

We have just ascended toward a pinnacle of heightened description that is now expanded to include "everything," completing the picture of paradise: "Huge salads,

cottage cheese, pinapple, plums, egg salad, prunes. . . ."
"Huge" reemphasizes the previous "vast" and "great,"
while words like "cottage" and "egg" provide a home-
spun effect. The repetition of *p* sounds glides into "vast
baked apples," which completes the image of expansion
and hints once again at Biblical Eden.

But then the completion of the circle, the down side
the Christian tradition's Wheel of Fortune is represented
by images of the fall—"tumbling dishes of grapes pale
green and brown." The passage contains images of collapse and death in fruit's unripe colors—vibrant as neon
is before. The fall is then represented linguistically
through a cascading heap of images: ". . . immense pans
of cheesecake, of raspberry cream cake, of flaky rich
Napoleons, of simple Boston cakes, armies of éclairs, of
enormously dark chocolate cake (gleaming scatalogical
brown). . . ." The "of" clauses provide bizarrely militar-
istic images of pastry, suggesting post-fall Western civilization by the apparently simple names of cakes. The
images are then made philosophical and deepened by
"of deepdish strudel, of time and the river," the latter
phrase the title of Thomas Wolfe's second novel.

After the "fall" come images of renewal, "of freshly
baked powdered cookies." A return to fruits of "glazed
strawberry-banana desserts—wild glazed orange cakes"
results in neon-like images that infer the possibility of
false appearances. Yet these images also introduce the
idea of building toward paradise: ". . .pyramiding glazed
desserts made of raspberries, whipcream, lady fingers
sticking up—vast sections reserved for the splendors of
coffee cakes and Danish crullers. . . ." Notice here the
rising shapes of "pyramids," "fingers," "up." At the same
time, the repetition of "vast" links this description to

those before and underscores an expansive feeling of "splendors." The celebration of the spiritual buildup toward heaven is the climax of the section: "rich mad milk" and "bread bun mountain" indicate structures building upward with purity, with "white" liquid running through.

Then a new counter is to be considered: "Then the serious business, the wild steaming fragrant hot-plate counter— Roast lamb, roast loin of pork, roast sirloin of beef, baked breast of lamb, stuff'd pepper, boiled chicken, stuff'd spring chicken, things to make the poor penniless mouth water. . . ." Again the oppositions of sounds and images, the rendering of key words in repetition, all contribute to speed and simultaneity, all moving toward the final image of joy and sadness combined at once: the interlocking phrasing initiated by the word "roast," the phrases that repeat images of meat in all fashions, the elision of "stuff'd," and the hotplate counter described as "fragrant" as if it were a flower garden.

The contrast initiated by the phrase "poor penniless" introduces "big sections of meat fresh from ovens, and a great knife sitting alongside and the server who daintily lays out portions as thin as paper." The suggestion is that the vision is merely a mirage laid out before the eyes and nose, but not for the taking. This vision is the vision of promise that is realized only by the elect. The profusion of images heap up: "The coffee counter, the urns, the cream jet, the steam," all culminating in the ultimate "shiny" food, the sweet counter: "But most of all it's that shining glazed sweet counter—showering like heaven—an all-out promise of joy in the great city of kicks."

The meaning is thus laid out like the food, in an illusion of plenty showering down with promise, an "American Dream" of infinite possibility. But the fulfillment of this promise is dependent upon true "greatness," not just "glaze" and tinsel. To this word flow Kerouac adds a postscript of further foods, but the point is already made. The final images bring the rhetorical tropes of the prose section full circle, but—as we might expect—not without the final view of Cody being rendered in the antithetical imagery of beat/angelic: "(Poor Cody, in front of this in his scuffled-up beat shoes, his literary 'imitation' suit he had wanted to wear to be acceptable in New York cafeterias which he thought would be brown and plain like Denver cafeterias, with ordinary food)." Cody's image is thus maintained as an outsider, a stranger to the city with his face pressed up against windows, observing without touching.

Kerouac had begun the setting of the novel in "an old diner like the ones Cody and his father ate in." Kerouac finally concludes that the smell of the old diner "is curiously the hungriest in America": "It is FOODY instead of just spicy, or—it's like dishwater soap just washed a pan of hamburg—nameless—memoried—sincere—makes the guts of men curl in October" (*VC*, 3–4). Hector's Cafeteria, then, is meant to contrast with the old diner as rival image of America.

The Geneology of the Hero

In *Visions of Cody*, the hero is fleshed out as the circular motif of the language becomes more refined. A long passage at the beginning of section 2 illustrates Kerouac's method:

Around the poolhalls of Denver during World War II a strange looking boy began to be noticeable to the characters who frequented the places afternoon and night and even to the casual visitors who dropped in for a game of snookers after supper when all the tables were busy in an atmosphere of smoke and great excitement and a continual parade passed in the alley from the backdoor of one poolroom on Glenarm Street to the backdoor of another—a boy called Cody Pomeray, the son of a Larimer Street wino. Where he came from nobody knew or at first cared. Older heroes of the other generations had darkened the walls of the poolhalls long before Cody got there; memorable eccentrics, great poolsharks, even killers, jazz musicians, traveling salesmen, anonymous frozen bums who came in on winter nights to sit an hour by the heat never to be seen again, among whom (and not to be remembered by anyone because there was no one there to keep a love check on the majority of the boys as they swarmed among themselves year by year with only casual but sometimes haunted recognition of faces, unless strictly local characters from around the corner) was Cody Pomeray, Sr. who in his hobo life that was usually spent stumbling in here and sat in the same old bench which was later to be occupied by his son in desperate meditations on life. (*VC*, 47–48)

This first prose paragraph of section 2 consists of two main sentences, long and all-inclusive, both of which swirl with added clauses without the relief of limitation and end-stop. The sonar and visual images carry the meaning and movement. The first sentence falls without breath to the first dash, which eclipses the subject, Cody, the son of a wino. Again the antithetical images juxtapose with one another in ironic contrast. This is, after all, a poolhall, an atmosphere of smoke and excitement where seedy "characters" congregate. In this setting the hero looks "strange" and "noticeable," even though the others are themselves "memorable eccentrics," "killers," "great poolsharks," "jazz musicians," "traveling salesmen," "bums." Central to the section is the idea that nobody knows where Cody comes from or cares. While Kerouac makes this illustration specific in colorful vocabulary, the actual images are shady and smoky like its subjects—"the haunted recognition of faces." Rather than aggrandize in the adjectival manner of the Hector's Cafeteria section, here the attributes of heroism are humble. The hero is contrasted with the father, who is "spent," and "stumbling." His son, on the other hand, fills his shoes "in desperate meditations on life." Kerouac's American hero is thus established in this seedy setting.

In the next paragraph, Kerouac suggests the look of the hero: "He looked like that Hollywood stunt man who is fist-fighting in place of the hero and has such a remote, furious, anonymous viciousness (one of the loneliest things in the world to see and we've all seen it a thousand times in a thousand B-movies) that everybody begins to be suspicious because they know the hero wouldn't act like that in real unreality" (*VC*, 48). Kerouac stresses the cinematic quality of the juxtaposed images by comparison with Hollywood B-movies. Again the appearance-and-reality motif emerges. This theme will take further prominence in the "Joan Rawshanks in the Fog" section, which actually takes place on a movie set. What is distinctive about the description of Cody here is that it lacks specific attributes but has a sense of generalization from the particular, as if Kerouac were looking at his subject through the eye of a camera and bringing the face into focus.

Kerouac finally sums up: "Nevertheless the face of a great hero—a face to remind you that the infant springs from the great Assyrian bush of a man, not from an eye, an ear or a forehead—the face of a Simón Bolívar, Robert E. Lee, young Whitman, young Melville, a statue in the park, rough and free" (*VC*, 49). Even here in the most specific part of the description, Kerouac generalizes from specific details of creation myths to make his heroics part of an overall creation myth. He thus substantiates the origins of the infant who comes into the world in a state of innocence, believing everything under his father's roof until he finds himself "wretched," "miserable," "poor," "blind," and "naked." With the visage of a "gruesome grieving ghost" he goes "shuddering through nightmare life" (*OR*, 105). The primary raison d' être of this description is Kerouac's overall concern with the establishment of a hero that is America itself. The epithet, "rough and free," describes with greater clarity the idea Kerouac has, not only of the heroic persona, but of America, the writer/self, and language.

The creation of this hero thus becomes the central preoccupation of this spiraling narrative. The antithetical images achieve meaning through the simultaneous presentation of their range of possibility, ignoring contradictions and, in fact, embracing them. The hero goes on to be described as an emblem of America. Indeed, one of the most important attractions to the Dean/Cody persona for Kerouac was that he represented a raw American spirit. Images of building/collapsing are characteristic of this section, as part of the establishment of his nature as hero. Thus Cody's character extends Kerouac's idea of America from the imagery of *The Town and the City* and *On the Road*.

The following flashback account of the hero illustrates how Kerouac's language changes in tone to present the antithetical imagery of Cody's early life: "So it was as though Cody Pomeray's early life was haunted by the sooty girders and worn old black planks of railroad bridges behind warehouses, by cinder yards where great concentrations of cardboard crates that were a nuisance to foremen of factories became the sly opportunity of bums . . ." (*VC*, 78). The tone is much less that of *exclamatio* and much more that of the litany, as if the revelation of the general through these specific details of sound and visual sense expresses the lost innocence explained before. Solid structures are introduced and repeated: "girders," "planks," "bridges," "warehouses," "crates," "factories"—the homely images of industry, of structures going up. These are, however, undercut by opposing images of "sooty," "worn," "black," "cinder," "bums." The notion here is not the expansive vision of America, but, as we might expect, the notion of limitation as seen in the idea that "bridges"—transitions— are obscured by "warehouses," that structures are a "nuisance" to men, that "factories" give bums the opportunity to be "sly." "So" introduces this writing as if it were saga. The patterns of vowels are disconcerting, not smooth, and the alliteration of hard *k* ("concentrations of cardboard crates") and *f* ("foremen of factories") sounds contain the foreboding sense of life being "haunted."

The image then switches to a description of downtown, quite literally "down" town, with its repeated bridge images undercut by "disaster":

... the backplaces of what we call downtown, the nameless
tunnels, alleys, sidings, platforms, ramps, ash heaps, minia-
ture dumps, unofficial parking lots fit for murders, the filthy
covered-with-rags plazas that you can see at the foot of great
redbrick chimneys—the same chimney that had bemused Cody
on many a dreaming afternoon when he looked at it toppling
forward as clouds upswept the air in readiness for the big
disaster. . . . (VC, 78)

The redbrick and chimneys, which have come to be identified with America, once again become part of the imagery of building/collapsing, along with other structures
of building or transition such as "tunnels," "alleys," "sidings," "platforms," "ramps," "heaps," "dumps," "lots."
These images later are opposed by images of "murder,"
"filthy," "toppling," "disaster." As these images become
more pronounced, they take hold of Kerouac's (through
Cody's) imagination, because, as I have already shown,
Cody goes beyond the legacy of his father, the wino bum,
by dreaming and meditating on life. He thus carries
the burden of consciousness that makes the "vision" of
the solid structures of America yield up an "unreal
reality."

The blurring of the distinction between appearance
and reality, between concrete structures and the trappings of dreams, supplies another set of antithetical oppositions and also gives the writing a surreal quality. As
the prose becomes more meditative, the contemplation
of the universe is meant to signify a change in consciousness from one level of understanding to the next:
"These things had been the necessary parts of his first
universe, its furniture, just as the little rich boy in a blue
playsuit in some swank suburb outside St. Louis
stands . . ." (VC, 78). Here the deliberate juxtaposition

of appearance with reality emerges through the concrete, homely, seedy structures of life that are coupled
with the hypothetical American dream vision of the little
boy. His universe, the entire world which he knows, is
one of mere trappings and furnishings, structures I have
already identified. The alliteration of "suit in some swank
suburb outside St. Louis stands" almost hisses as ironic
contrast to the chimneys and other props of Cody's own
cityscape environment. This effective opposition exists
simultaneously with a dream-vision generalization:

... in November, beneath the bleak black branches, staring
at a universe which is necessarily and unalterably furnished
with things like half-timbered English style housefronts, circular wooded drives for avenue blocks, forests of birch, the
wire fencing in back of Tudor garages, boxer dogs, bicycles,
sleek autos reposant at dusk before the warm lights that shine
behind the drapes of a Spanish style house worth twenty-eight
thousand dollars bought by an insurance broker who cuts
along the narrow redbrick downtown streets of St. Louis near
the markets by day.... (VC, 78)

Cutting through the rude images of Cody's reality are
the more genteel dream images that exist simultaneously
with them, "beneath the bleak black branches." He looks
at structures ("things," "housefronts," "blocks," "forests,"
"garages") connected by conduits ("drives," "fencing,"
"bicycles," "autos") that either join, or give access to, or
set limits to, the concrete structures in question. While
these structures and conduits are still images of building,
the light that shines behind them indicates the impermanence that marks the scene. This is the meaning of
the all-inclusive imagery in this passage (as it is in the
Hector's Cafeteria section). Structures, usually solid and

permanent, will collapse and, in fact, already have the seeds of that collapse within them. The light that shines through drapes further indicates that what appears permanent in the structure of the fine Spanish-style house will collapse. The seeds of that collapse reside with the "insurance broker," a typically American character who personifies the idea of security and permanence, "narrow" by virtue of the vision of "redbrick downtown streets"—the very conduits through which he moves through the day, unsuspecting and unconfronted by the "nightmare life" of Cody's consciousness with which it is juxtaposed.

The life of the hero moves on:

Cody's life in Denver entered a second phase and this one had for its background, its prime focal goal, the place to which he was forever rushing, the place his father had only known as a bum in meek stumbling uplooking approach or had more vigorously known in his youth but that was Des Moines and long ago, nothing less and nothing more than the redbrick wall behind the red neons: it was everywhere in Denver where he went and everywhere in America all his life where he was. (*VC*, 78–79)

A summation of the progress of the hero is supplied here, even though the passage occurs in the middle of the extremely long exposition of the origins of the hero. First, the idea of levels is continued in the notion of "phase," as Cody is "forever rushing." The mention of his father as a bum, "uplooking," gives the sense of Cody's separation from his background through the quality of his vision, the focal point of the book, as is ascertained even by the title. But, at the same time, the notion of looking at all ties him to his sordid past. Second, the phrase "nothing less and nothing more" indicates the integrity of the complete image that is created by the antithetical properties of Kerouac's myth: neon images give way to the solid structures of walls behind them, and this lighting reveals a point of consciousness that is larger than the hero or any point in his universe. Behind the structure of Kerouac's language is the insight he gains through Cody as to the nature of the oppositions building/collapsing, appearance/reality, expansion/limitation, happiness/sadness: America in its structure (its values) and spirit (even though haunted) is thus depicted through its hero, Cody.

The Hero's Voice

Because Cody remains the basic symbol of Kerouac's insight, he also becomes Kerouac's model for expression of that insight. The section that follows, "Frisco: The Tape," shows Cody's interaction with Jack Duluoz, the narrator's persona. The section is quite literally a transcription of a taped conversation between the two, an experiment which attempts to erase the "fiction" of narrative form entirely. Tytell says that *Visions of Cody* is "the grand register of how Cassady affected the Beats with the kinesis of being and an appreciation of the cataclysmic import of the here and now. Cassady was . . . the model of the common urge to communicate ordinary experience in a natural, unpretentious voice.[10] An examination of the section, however, makes clear that the conversation is actually a discourse in aesthetic methodology, beginning with Jack saying "And during the night he said 'I'm an artist!' " (*VC*, 119). This contrasts with the activities of ordinary people such as the insurance broker, who only "cuts along the redbrick downtown streets" during the day.

Cody is, of course, a catalyst for the expression of the Beat vision. In Cody's words: "Used to not feel couple of years ago hardly worth it to complete the sentence and then it got so try as I might I couldn't and it developed into something that way, see, so now in place of that I just complete the thought whatever I've learned . . . instead of trying to make myself hurry back to where I should be . . ." (*VC,* 145). This is another way of explaining the nonlinearity of *Visions of Cody:* the progression of the novel spirals up rather than moves and develops progressively and consecutively. In another sense, Kerouac plumbs the dimensions of the Cassady legend by working over the material of the Beat experience on the tape, and recognizing the importance of the language in which it is remembered: "I go on talking *about* these things, thinking about things, and memory, 'cause we're both concerned about, ah memory, and just relax like Proust. . . . So I talk on about that as the mind . . . remembers and thinks and that's why it's difficult . . ." (*VC,* 146).

The antithetical images the mind produces when it freely creates a vocabulary for memory reveals the virtues of taped conversations: one always knows "when sharply to cut the knife . . . and switch back to something . . ." (*VC,* 146). Cody's language is thus described as "unpunctuated talk." The tone of the talk, however, is punctuated by breath. As the speakers move through the various aspects of the Beat experience interspersed with personal renderings of history and philosophy, the language becomes more engaging than the elements upon which it reflects.

The section will probably endure most easily as a kind of literary criticism in bop. Though the narrator and his subject constantly talk about the act of writing with reference to writers of the past, their conversation is at the same time an attempt to explore possibilities for contemporary writing. The writing looks like a dialogue:

Jack. . . . look at this sentence. (flute) Now. Concerning . . . THE TAPE RECORDER IS TURNING, THE TYPE-WRITER IS WAITING, AND I SIT HERE WITH A FLUTE IN MY MOUTH. And so you're just sittin here thinking while it's playing (plays flitty flute)

Cody. That's just what I've been doin but I couldn't think of the thought. And I guess the reason I can't think of it and why I'm blocked is because I didn't formalize it or I didn't think about it long enough, soon as the thought hit me, why, I didn't think it out, because I was gonna blurt it out. Damn, if I'd have just spoken—(*Cody running water at sink, flute blowing, watery flute*) Your coffee's gettin cold. *I'll* bring it over but I don't know which one it is (*really meant, he says, he didn't know whether I wanted cream or sugar or what*). (*VC,* 154)

The "Imitation of the Tape" section that follows reads like a long interior monologue. Duluoz calls it "this movie house of mine in the dream" (*VC,* 251). Here he creates a variety of voices—for example, Lady Godiva talking about Jack Duluoz and ending her monologue with a conjecture on composition: "Let us ascertain, in the morning, if there is a way of abstracting the interesting paragraphs of material in all this running consciousness stream that can be used as the progressing lightning chapters of a great essay about the wonders of the world as it continually flashes up in retrospect . . ." (*VC*, 258). Though Kerouac tries to experiment with language like a tape recorder in the attempt to erase the "fiction" of narrative altogether, he cannot, of course, completely accomplish his desired fictional mode. His self-consciousness about the subject of writing is a trope which gathers greater momentum in these linguistic experiments. The narrative is so absorbed in the philosophy of writing, it merely establishes a mode by which the book as a whole can be understood, without the release of language that exemplifies a sustained excellence. Instead, without the refinement of the writer's standard revision process, there is no way of "abstracting the interesting paragraphs." The preoccupation with writing itself prevents Kerouac from achieving completely his cherished aim.

Hollywood and the American Dream

The "Joan Rawshanks in the Fog" section in a sense completes the book, because there is no separation between the description of the set and the transition into the concluding prose sections. The ending, however, reveals the synthesis of the rhetorical tropes that were introduced in the earlier novels of the legend and the techniques Kerouac discovers through his experimentation here. According to Carolyn Cassady, Kerouac wrote this section after he turned a corner in Hollywood and happened to observe the actress Joan Crawford on a movie set.[11] The Crawford movie set he describes fits in neatly with his own preoccupations of viewing life as a movie and of working with juxtaposing images (cinematic montage), as well as with his great concern with the general problem of appearance and reality I have mentioned earlier in this chapter.

But the Crawford movie set is completely transformed by the language of simultaneous apprehension of all its possibilities. Again, Kerouac's aesthetic solution for the enactment of simultaneity in action is evident in the opening scene of the section:

Joan Rawshanks stands alone in the fog. Her name is Joan Rawshanks and she knows it, just as anybody knows his name, and she knows who she is, same way, Joan Rawshanks stands alone in the fog and a thousand eyes are fixed on her in all kinds of ways; above Joan Rawshanks rises the white San Francisco apartment house in which the terrified old ladies who spend their summers in lake resort hotels are now wringing their hands in the illuminated (by the floodlights outside) gloom of their livingrooms, some of them having Venetian blinds in them but none drawn; Joan Rawshanks leans her head in her hands, she's wearing a mink coat by the wet bushes, she leans against the dewy wire fence separating the slopeyard of the magnificent San Francisco DeLuxe Arms from the neat white Friscoan street-driveway sloping abruptly at seventy-five degrees; in back where the angry technicians muster and make gestures in the blowing fog that rushes past klieg lights and ordinary lights in infinitesimal cold showers, to make everything seem miserable and storm-hounded, as though we were all on a mountain top saving the brave skiers in the howl of the elements, but also just like the lights and the way the night mist blows by them at the scene of great airplane disasters or train wrecks or even just construction jobs that have reached such a crucial point that there's overtime in muddy midnight Alaskan conditions; Joan Rawshanks, wearing a mink coat, is trying to adjust herself to the act of crying but has a thousand eyes of local Russian Hill spectators who've been hearing about the Hollywood crew filming for the last hour, ever since dinner's end, and are arriving on the scene here despite the fog (move over from my microphone wire, there) in driblets; pretty girls with fresh dew fog faces and bandanas and moonlit (though no moon) lips; also old people who customarily at this hour make grumpy shows of walking the dog in dismal and empty slope streets of the rich and magnificently quiet; the fog of San Francisco in the night, as a buoy in the bay goes b-o, as a buoy in the bag goes b-o, bab-o, as a buoy in the bag goes bab-o. . . . (*VC,* 275–76)

The sounds and visual images in this passage are well integrated; the jazz motif Kerouac has been using all along now has a correlative in the visual arts, but actually surpasses the medium of film in rendering simultaneity. Kerouac's panoramic view of the Joan Crawford movie set is an all-inclusive take. Beginning with the "jewel center," the introduction of the actress herself, Kerouac here includes a female image to his collection of proletariat types in the *Book of Dreams*—she "stands alone." Kerouac establishes her identity in the curious way in which he has also identified his hero, Cody, in a matrix of impressions—tropes of synaesthesia, synchronicity, and syncopation—with the repetition of her name, Joan Rawshanks, as a narrative refrain. The actress's name is repeated in a circular motif throughout the description until the final reduction of language to mere syllables. This language play prefigures, as I shall show, the key segments of *Desolation Angels.*

In the second invocation of Joan Rawshanks, she not only stands alone, but a "thousand eyes are fixed on her in all kinds of ways," providing the mandala effect we observed in the Hector's Cafeteria scene. From this circle, Kerouac's camera eye pans upward into a digression

that stands in opposition to the posturing of the actress—
the old ladies are "terrified" and "wringing their hands."
They are, however, illuminated—as before, Kerouac is
interested in the uses of light—by "floodlights," which
now acquire connotations of the Biblical, even the an-
tediluvian. It is gloom, however, that is illuminated, which
in turn sets up the antithetical images of ecstasy/sadness.
The gloom is also tied linguistically to the "living rooms"
whose Venetian blinds set up another opposition of light/
dark.

In the third mention of Joan Rawshanks, she no longer
stands but "leans," her motions following those of the
old ladies, "her head in her hands," "wearing a mink
coat by the wet bushes." Through a masterful use of
synaesthesia, the fur coat itself becomes "wet" or glossy,
especially as Rawshanks leans against a dewy fence. The
fence is now used to draw the parameters of the frame
by separating the "magnificent" from the "neat and
white." The antithetical images are thus those of glam-
orous/humble, heightened/plain.

Then the eye once again focuses on Joan Rawshanks,
wearing the mink coat as a kind of epithet. The scene
begins to infect her performance as she tries to give the
appearance of crying to all the eyes around her. The
opposition of "moon" and "no moon" introduces the
antithetical imagery of "pretty girls" as they are juxtaposed with old people, rendered in turn through the
rude images of "grumpy," "dog," "dismal," "empty." Their
"slope streets" oppose those streets that are "rich and
magnificently quiet." The image has come full circle.

The circular structure of this all-inclusive passage prefigures the prose structures of *Desolation Angels* as it exemplifies the growing perfection of Kerouac's writing

style. As for the development of Kerouac's legend, a movie actress is a natural symbol of the Hollywood hyperbole that Kerouac was weaned on and that comes to depict the American Dream. What he learns from his experience, especially from figures in his life like Neal Cassady (the model for Cody), is, however, an opposition to the Hollywood view of America.

Like the dream ending of *On the Road,* Duluoz departs from Cody in a deeply elegiac, even litanous tone, reminiscent of Milton's resurrection of his friend Edward King in "Lycidas": "Adios, you who watched the sun go down, at the rail, by my side, smiling—

Adios, King" (*VC,* 398)

In *Visions of Cody,* Kerouac finds the style appropriate to his ideas about language and solves the problem of the technique through the analogy with music. Still, this refinement will be realized to a greater extent in *Desolation Angels,* which will complete the core of the entire legend. Kerouac thus escapes the linear route mapped out in *On the Road.* The language of *Visions of Cody* allows him to slip out of reality into the creative dreams through which he can envision the darkness to which he is so attracted. Yet the writer/self requires one more permutation to achieve this escape fully. It emerges at last in *Desolation Angels,* where Kerouac completes this adventure through a more developed sense of the rhetorical solution adumbrated in *Visions of Cody.*

5

The Sound of Despair:
A Perfected Nonlinearity

Do you hear that? The sound of it alone is wonderful, no?
What can you give me in English to match that for sheer
beauty of resonance?

Henry Miller
The Colossus of Maroussi

KEROUAC ATTEMPTED to resolve the aesthetic
problems of *Visions of Cody* in his next period of
writing, from 1953 with the writing of *The Subterraneans*
on through the sixties, as his life and thinking became
more religious and philosophical. The culmination of
the experiments that comprise *Visions of Cody* is found
in *Desolation Angels,* a novel concerned with the period
of legend/life from 1956 to 1957. The novel, first published in 1965, is based on Kerouac's journals written in
the year before the appearance of *On the Road;* these
writings were put in novel form after the success of *On
the Road,*[1] and integrate the events of the road with the
Zen philosophy he was learning as he developed both
as a man and as a writer. The first half of the book was
completed in Mexico City in October 1956 and "typed

up" in 1957; the second half was not written until 1961, although chronologically it follows immediately after the first.[2] The novel is thus another take on Kerouac's road adventures: it covers roughly the same aspects of his legend as *On the Road* and *Visions of Cody* and is stylistically the logical culmination of them both.

Although the merits of this novel have often been hinted at, some critics, such as Dennis McNally, state flatly that the writing is not nearly Kerouac's best.[3] Tytell, on the other hand, lauds the work as "the best existing account of the lives of the Beats" and further claims that its influence upon the nonfiction novel emerges in such books as Tom Wolfe's *Electric Kool-Aid Acid Test*. Tytell also groups *Desolation Angels* with *The Dharma Bums* in claiming that neither novel represents the essential Kerouac—the ideal of spontaneous composition, the flaunting of conventional novelistic expectations.[4]

Indeed, *Desolation Angels* has not yet been understood as a stylistically integrated work. If the earlier experimental novel combines adventure with the meditative mode, then the later novel builds upon that combined form by sustaining the structure, techniques, and images beyond the initial experimentalism. If *On the Road* describes the outward journey and *Visions of Cody* the inner one, here the techniques of both are joined for a more consistent narrative. Thus, even though several books follow in the chronological sequence of Kerouac's career, *Desolation Angels* will be shown here to be the stylistic perfection of the techniques of the Duluoz legend, and perhaps its best expression.

The circular narrative structure of *Desolation Angels* begins and ends with a period of intense confrontation with the self. The terror and beauty of utter solitude on

Desolation Peak—sixty-three days of proximity to nature's powers, including lightning storms, huge looming mountains, voids of gorges and canyons, bright sunsets, fog, silence, loneliness—end with Duluoz/Kerouac's finding nothingness at the bottom of "myself abysmal," after the lustful desire to return to the world.[5] In the end he finds only "a peaceful sorrow at home is the best I'll ever be able to offer the world, in the end, and so I told my Desolation Angels goodbye. A new life for me" (*DA*, 366). Ironically, the descent from the heights of the mountain provides for the ascent of the writer's spirit. Opposing images once again define the thematic shape as well as the linguistic component of Kerouac's text. And the return to the self follows from it full circle.

Kerouac's ability to integrate the diverse components of his prose emerges at last in a distinct narrative voice. More highly evolved than the Paradise or Duluoz narrators of the previous books, this Duluoz voice provides a consistent method of discourse for each prose segment. Each division—whether book, part, or section—echoes the circular shape of the whole, with the opposition between the "abysmal self" and the world vast and teeming with "angels" magnified. The Dean/Cody persona is no longer needed as a catalyst for the narrator's philosophical and adventuring self. The Duluoz narrator here is thus more developed, integrated, and self-contained.

As a self-conscious persona, Kerouac's narrator shapes the action of the novel through his perception. Kerouac now achieves greater control of his method in the reflexive connection between the act of living and the act of writing. Most important, Kerouac's command of his spontaneous prose technique has developed through his experience. The disclosures of *Desolation Angels* are really the revision of initial insights recorded in *On the Road* and *Visions of Cody.* This revision is now his methodological control.

The circular shape of his local discourse controls the design of his narrative at large. Thus the overall form is but the largest circle of these interior structures of thought, the prose paragraphs that comprise the whole. The book and part divisions are named and numbered and the sections are numbered; but even though they are therefore sequential and cannot be transposed as was the case in *Visions of Cody,* the book and part divisions nonetheless follow the familiar romantic circle. "Desolation Angels," the first book, contains two parts—"Desolation in Solitude" and "Desolation in the World"— indicating the linguistic polarities of Kerouac's thought in this final stage of legend. "Passing Through," the second book, has four part divisions in which the writer/ self defined in the first book becomes a transient being (like the "gruesome grieving ghost" identified in the earlier fiction) who is "Passing Through Mexico," "Passing Through New York," "Passing Through Tangiers, France and London," and "Passing Through America Again." Structurally and thematically, then, there is a beginning in innocence that must pass through experience. The Higher Innocence that Kerouac characteristically desires can only be accomplished by the return to themes that are American.

It will be worthwhile to see what this writer/self has to say about his enlightenment in order to describe fully the circular journey as well as to see how the creation of the narrator follows the precepts of Kerouac's earlier literary ethic: "And now, after the experience on top of the mountain where I was alone for two months without being questioned or looked at by any single human being I began a complete turnabout in my feelings about life. . . . I knew now that my life was a search for peace as an artist, but not only as an artist—As a man of contemplations . . . "(*DA*, 219). Jack Duluoz sees himself as singular, lonely, and separate. He talks about the circular notion of a "turnabout" following the movement down from the mountain. This movement echoes the shape of the entire work structurally and thematically.

"A man of contemplations" further defines the consistency of mood of *Desolation Angels*, a contemplative mood which Kerouac only now achieves: "I was searching for a peaceful kind of life dedicated to contemplation and the delicacy of that, for the sake of my art (in my case prose, tales) (narrative rundowns of what I saw and how I saw) but I also searched for this as my way of life, that is, to see the world from the viewpoint of solitude and to meditate upon the world without being imbroglio'd in its actions . . ." (*DA*, 220). Here is another circumlocution that develops in more detail his notion of the writer/self. The contemplation initiates a down movement, as if in his thoughts he were still perched above on the mountain. The word "rundown" resonates, as does the manifest integration of life and art in solitude. But most important of all is Kerouac's declaration (through Duluoz) that his life is dedicated to the contemplation of the creation of not only "what I saw" (a minor explanation of his interest in the form of description called sketching), but also "how I saw" (that is, the vehicle of perception in language). The legend reaches its fullness, in other words, as a discovery of language.

The language of the writer/self is made up of rhetorical tropes similar to those we have found in the earlier novels, revealing an integrity of preoccupation as well as a more highly-evolved form. The free prose sections of the *Visions of Cody* experiment become a harmonious sphere in the novel's three-dimensional atmosphere, as once again a musical analogy provides a solution to structural problems. Duluoz explains his control over the material in the following way: " 'There's a certain amount of control going on [in my writing] like a man telling a story in a bar without interruptions or even one pause' " (*DA*, 280).

The voice of *Desolation Angels* is especially appropriate to Kerouac's interior journey as a rhetorical spiral leads him from exuberance to despair. A hymnal, litanous language maintains the musical analogy. Thus Kerouac solves the time/space, linear/nonlinear problems encountered in the earlier novels because chord structures—or, in the linguistic register, "narrative rundowns"—allow him to repeat as well as to progress. The effect is the paradox of circular motion, at times a mandala of themes on a circular plane. The spiral of recurrence and progression provides the familiar circular motion from beat to beatitude: "It's *béat,* it's the beat to keep, it's the beat of the heart, it's being beat and down in the world and like oldtime lowdown and like in ancient civilizations the slave boatmen rowing galleys to a beat and servants spinning pottery to a beat" (*DA,* 123). The juxtaposition of antithetical images in earlier works is now the very subject of Kerouac's prose. Here the matrix of rhetorical tropes is, as I shall show, simultaneously the completion of an entire image in all its possibilities. The beat moves from a staccato rhythm of exuberance in terse phrasing, through the images of "down in the world" and "oldtime lowdown," to longer, more cumbersome descriptions of mundane labors usually associated with human misery. Thus Kerouac uses the preoccupations and themes of the entire legend with a more masterful command of the material as his mind recollects it in memory.

Desolation in Solitude

A detailed account of the elements of Kerouac's circles will illustrate this solitude in action. Several sections of prose will be analyzed to explain Kerouac's mature methodology. Indeed, the language of *Desolation Angels* will be shown to be Kerouac's highest expression of "free prose."

In section 2 of "Desolation in Solitude," Duluoz explains why he is on Desolation Peak and has to stare at it for over seventy days. Contained within the passage are suggestions of the madness of solitude, especially in the allusions to King Lear on the heath. At times, the language reflects the garbled and mangled musings of a man in painful isolation; his speech in inchoate syllables of suffering reflects his inability to express these feelings coherently. At these times, the sounds themselves control the narrative. In toto, the section reads like a dramatic monologue:

Yes, for I'd thought, in June, hitch hiking up there to the Skagit Valley in northwest Washington for my fire lookout job "When I get to the top of Desolation Peak and everybody leaves on mules and I'm alone I will come face to face with God or Tathagata and find out once and for all what is the meaning of all this existence and suffering and going to and fro in vain" but instead I'd come face to face with myself, no liquor, no drugs, no chance of faking it but face to face with ole Hateful Duluoz Me and many's the time I thought I die, suspire of boredom, or jump off the mountain, but the days, nay the hours dragged and I had no guts for such a leap, I had to *wait* and get to see the face of reality—and it finally comes that afternoon of August 8 as I'm pacing in the high alpine yard on the little wellworn path I'd beaten, in dust and rain, on many a night, with my oil lamp banked low inside the cabin with the four-way windows and peaked pagoda roof and lightning rod point, it finally comes to me, after even tears, and gnashing, and the killing of a mouse and attempted murder of another, something I'd never done in my life (killing animals even rodents), it comes in these words: "The void is not disturbed by any kind of ups and downs, my God look at Hozomeen, is he worried or tearful? Does he bend before storms or snarl when the sun shines or sigh in the late day drowse? Does he smile? Was he not born out of madbrained turmoils and upheavals of raining fire and now's Hozomeen and nothing else? Why should I choose to be bitter or sweet, he does neither?—Why cant I be like Hozomeen and O Platitude O hoary old platitude of the bourgeois mind "take life as it comes"—Twas that alcoholic biographer, W. E. Woodward, said, "There's nothing to life but just the living of it"—But O God I'm bored! But is Hozomeen bored? And I'm sick of words and explanations. Is Hozomeen?

> Aurora Borealis
> over Hozomeen—
> The void is stiller

—Even Hozomeen'll crack and fall apart, nothing lasts, it is only a faring-in-that-which-everything-is, a passing-through, that's what's going on, why ask questions or tear hair or weep, the burble blear purple Lear on his moor of woes he is only a gnashy old flap with winged whiskers beminded by a fool— to be *and* not to be, that's what we are—Does the Void take any part in life and death? does it have funerals? or birth cakes? why not I be like the Void, inexhaustibly fertile, beyond serenity, beyond even gladness, just Old Jack (and not even that) and conduct my life from this moment on (though winds blow through my windpipe), this ungraspable image in a crystal ball is not the Void, the Void is the crystal ball itself and all my woes the Lankavatara Scripture hairnet of fools, "Look sirs, a marvelous sad hairnet"—Hold together, Jack, pass through everything, and everything is one dream, one appearance, one flash, one sad eye, one crystal lucid mystery, one word—Hold still, man, regain your love of life and go down from this mountain and simply *be*—*be*—be the infinite fertilities of the one mind of infinity, make no comments, complaints, criticisms, appraisals, avowals, sayings, shooting stars of thought, just *flow, flow,* be you all, be you what it is, it is only what it always is—Hope is a word like a snow-drift—This is the Great Knowing, this is the Awakening, this is the Voidness— So shut up, live, travel, adventure, bless and dont be sorry— Prunes, prune, eat your prunes— And you have been forever, and will be forever, and all the worrisome smashings of your foot on innocent cupboard doors it was only the Void pretending to be a man pretending not to know the Void—

I come back into the house a new man.

All I have to do is wait 30 long days to get down from the rock and see sweet life again—knowing it's neither sweet nor bitter but just what it is, and so it is—

So long afternoons I sit in my easy (canvas) chair facing Void Hozomeen, the silence hushes in my little shack, my stove is still, my dishes glitter, my firewood (old sticks that are the form of water and welp, that I light small Indian fires with in my stove, to make quick meals) my firewood lies piled and snaky in the corner, my canned goods wait to be opened, my old cracked shoes weep, my pans lean, my dish rags hang, my various things sit silent around the room, my eyes ache, the wind wallows and belts at the window and upped shutters, the light in late afternoon shades and bluedarks Hozomeen (revealing his streak of middle red) and there's nothing for me to do but wait—and breathe (and breathing is difficult in the thin high air, with West Coast sinus wheezings)—wait, breathe, eat, sleep, cook, wash, pace, watch, never any forest fires—and daydream, "What will I do when I get to Frisco? Why first thing I'll get a room in Chinatown"—but even nearer and sweeter I daydream what I'll do Leaving Day, some hallowed day in early September, "I'll walk down the trail, two hours, meet Phil in the boat, ride to the Ross Float, sleep there a night, chat in the kitchen, start early in the morning on the Diablo Boat, go right from that little pier (say hello to Walt), hitch right to Marblemount, collect my pay, pay my debts, buy a bottle of wine and drink it by the Skagit in the afternoon, and leave next morning for Seattle"—and on, down to Frisco, then L. A., then Nogales, then Guadalajara, then Mexico City— And still the Void is still and'll never move—

But I will be the Void, moving without having moved. (*DA*, 4–6)

Like every section, this one is a microcosm of the whole work, a compendium of antithetical imagery, a prose poem complete within itself. Placed at the book's beginning, this passage sets up the idea of the quest in solitude and without movement, reminiscent in its way of the gnomic utterances of the Old English "Seafarer" poem of which Ezra Pound was so fond. Kerouac uses the solitude of the American landscape, so profoundly frightening in its accentuation of his own preoccupations about life, to eclipse his own expression, his own self. The linguistic oppositions that unified earlier novels recur as animation is pared away and he is left alone, all the wandering "to and fro" supplanted by stillness. In the austere clearing that remains, the two principal Kerouacean techniques of vision are particularly evident: the all-inclusiveness of opposing imagery and the generalization from the particular to make a philosophical point.

Duluoz begins with a rhetorical "yes" of affirmation and proceeds to build up to a philosophical dialogue

with himself. Words like "up," "top," "peak," are count-
ered by "valley"; he suggests he must go up to stay level.
In his first speech to himself, he speaks of lateral movement which balances up and down. He begins the narrative refrain of "face to face," for example, and balances
that with "to and fro" for the creation of the tautologies
that are characteristic of this section. The narrative takes
a turn with "but," and between the repetitions of "face
to face" he begins a series of negations to counterpoint
the "yes" at the start: "no liquor, no drugs, no chance
of faking it. . . ." The first tautology of "face to face" is
"Hateful Duluoz Me," a self-negating image followed by
verbs that suggest his death: "I thought I die, suspire
of boredom, or jump off the mountain. . . ."

After the first break, indicated by dashes, concrete
details bring reality home. The word "and" precipitates
the all-inclusiveness of oppositions. "Wellworn," "beaten,"
"banked low" contrast with "peaked pagoda roof and
lightning rod point." Extreme actions, even when re-
ferring to mice, contrast with a simultaneous stasis: "The
void is not disturbed by any kind of ups and downs,"
Duluoz muses. He then identifies the Void and the mystery of the experience on Desolation Peak with another
mountain vision which he can actually sight from his
perch, a vision of Hozomeen, which becomes the object
of a set of rhetorical questions from which he generalizes. He questions the oppositions of "bitter or sweet,"
for example, and asks why we must choose between
them. Then, in further tautologies, he reveals that no
choices can be made because every choice already contains its own opposite anyway.

Kerouac's haiku in midsection is typical of *Desolation
Angels*,[6] and is a compressed form of his philosophizing

in general. Here the idea that the endurance of the mountain is second to the endurance of the Void is central to the linguistic collapse of oppositions, to the unified vision of all-inclusiveness. The next segment suggests that even the mountain will crack and fall apart, since "Nothing lasts." Again, Kerouac suggests a lateral movement of activity which goes along with the extreme stasis, boredom, and stillness of the mountain ("faring-in-that-which-everything-is" and "passing-through"), which is then set in opposition with the desire to "ask," "tear," "weep," echoing Prufrock's dilemma. The next cluster of mere syllables evokes Shakespeare ("burble blear purple Lear on his moor of woes"). Not only does Kerouac's narrator liken himself to Lear, but he generalizes from the comparison to the human condition as a whole—to be a "flap with winged whiskers beminded by a fool."

Then, evoking Shakespeare once more, he revises a tautology into "to be *and* not to be," with special emphasis upon the "and." Consciously or not, Kerouac strives for a stasis or balance of oppositions, leading to a series of questions about the activity of the Void—"Does the Void take any part in life and death? does it have funerals? or birth cakes?"—which ends in a single question, identifying the narrator in the negative: "Why not I be like the Void, inexhaustibly fertile, beyond serenity, beyond even gladness, just old Jack (and not even that)." The Void is represented in images of passing through: "beyond serenity," and "beyond gladness." Even Jack and non-Jack are represented with the same strong metaphor: "winds blow through my windpipe." Then he negates the Void to affirm himself. The oxymoron "ungraspable image" is used to define the Void and the "crystal ball"; the "hairnet of fools" is that by which he is "beminded" (like Lear above) when he preoccupies himself with his woes. Thus he brings the Lear image full circle. The net contains the hair torn away by man in despair. But it is a reassurance that allows the narrator to transcend the conceits of these tautologies by exhorting himself to have the courage to pass through.

First he tells himself to "hold together . . . everything," whether "dream," "appearance," "flash," "eye," "crystal lucid mystery," or finally, "word." He thus exhorts his writer/self to "hold still" and to "go down"—that is, to descend in order to ascend. This action results in "infinite fertilities," a correspondence with the "inexhaustibly fertile" nature of the Void earlier in the passage. And rather than create thoughts or words that prevent the passing through from taking place, he exhorts himself to "*flow.*" This exhortation precipitates another set of tautologies as the old ones break down: "It is only what it always is"; "Hope is a word like a snow-drift"; "This is the Great Knowing"; "[T]his is the Awakening"; "This is the Voidness." Thus Kerouac implements the "flow." And just as the appearance/reality theme is resolved in the me/not me imagery of *Desolation Angels*, the antithetical images brought "face to face" bring the picture of the Void full circle with its image of "pretending to be a man pretending not to know the Void." This writing, as if in Kerouac's characteristic "semi-trance" has thus built up to a release of expression—to the completion of an all-inclusive image.

There follows a return to Duluoz's physical state, with new understanding. That is, insight follows release: "I come back into the house a new man." Now an interior landscape is juxtaposed with the exterior landscape of the first movement. But the interior is not the same after the new insight. "Bitter" and "sweet" are not oppositions but are together in "what it is." Thus the description, though specific in detail, generalizes from the particular to show the interior in a total image, not subject to flux. Lateral movement marks the passivity of the scene: "silence hushes," "stove is still," "dishes glitter," "firewood . . . lies piled and snaky in the corner." The stillness evokes the Edenic paradise of prebirth bliss for which Duluoz is nostalgic. Though the objects in this cabin are personified, the verbs indicate passivity: "canned goods wait," "pans lean," "dish rags hang," "things sit silent."

But there is still movement in this silent scene as the wind "wallows and belts . . . upped shutters," a movement indicating ascension after a going down. This movement leads to enlightenment, to images of passing through: "wait," "breathe," "eat," "sleep," "cook," "wash," "pace," "watch," "daydream." Kerouac capitalizes Leaving Day as if it were a day of celebration and exuberance, and in one long breath envisions the future in a kind of apocalypse of mundane images that brings the section full circle with the repetition of Skagit and other geographic detail; the repetition of "then" allows the enumeration to flow. The ultimate paradox of the circular imagery of all-inclusiveness then emerges: "And still the Void is still and'll never move." The flow which implies movement is so all-inclusive as to take up all space and need not operate in time at all. This is the final enlightenment of the passage. Duluoz ends, however, by identifying himself ("face to face") with the Void in the bridge: "But I will be the Void, moving without having moved." True to Kerouac's design, even this bridge that ends the section defies closure as it leads to the next.

Desolation in the World

The second part of the first book opposes "Desolation in Solitude" with "Desolation in the World." An examination of a sample section will reveal still another development in Kerouac's expression. For example, Kerouac's "sketch" of Seattle in section 52 bears the refrain of how hard it is to come off the mountain:

Seattles in the fog, burlesque shows, cigars and wines and papers in a room, fogs, ferries, bacon and eggs and toast in the morning—sweet cities below.

Down about where the heavy timber begins, big Ponderosas and russet all-trees, the air hits me nice, green Northwest, blue pine needles, fresh, the boat is cutting a swath in the nearer lake, it's going to beat me, but just keep on swinging, Marcus Magee— You've had falls before and Joyce made a word two lines long to describe it—
brabarackotawackomanashtopataratawackomanac!

We'll light three candles to three souls when we get there.

The trail, last halfmile, is worse, than above, the rocks, big, small, twisted ravines for your feet— Now I begin sobbing for myself, cursing of course— "It never ends!" is my big complaint, just like I'd thought in the door, "How can anything ever end? But this is only a Samsara-World-of-Suffering trail, subject to time and space, therefore must end, but my God it will never end!" and I come running and thwapping finally no more— For the first time I fall exhausted without planning.

And the boat is coming right in.

"Cant make it."

I sit there a long time, moody faced and finished— Wont do it— But the boat gets coming closer, it's like timeclock civilization, gotta get to work on time, like on the railroad, tho you cant make it you'll make it— It was blasted in the forges with iron vulcan might, by Poseidon and his heroes, by Zen Saints with swords of intelligence, by Master Frenchgod— I push myself up and try on— Every step wont do, it wont work, that my thighs hold it up's'mystery to me—plah—

Finally I'm loading my steps on ahead of me, like placing topheavy things on a platform with outstretched arms, the kind of strain you cant keep up—other than the bare feet (now battered with torn skin and blisters and blood) I could just plow and push down the hill, like a falling drunk almost falling never quite falling and if so would it hurt as much as my feet?—nu—gotta push and place each up-knee and down with the barbfoot on scissors of Blakean Perfidy with worms and howlings everywhere—dust—I fall on my knees.

Rest that way awhile and go on.

"Eh damn Eh maudit" I'm crying last 100 yards—now the boat's stopped and Fred whistles sharply, no a hoot, an Indian Hooo! which I answer with a whistle, with fingers in mouth— He settles back to read a cowboy book while I finish that trail— Now I dont want him to hear me cry, but he does he must hear my slow sick steps—plawrp, plawrp—timber tinker of pebbles plopping off a rock round precipice, the wild flowers dont interest me no more—

"I cant make it" is my only thought as I keep going, which thought is like phosphorescent negative red glow imprinting the film of my brain "Gotta make it"—

> Desolation, Desolation
> so hard
> To come down off of. (*DA*, 76–77)

Again the passage is made up of antithetical imagery with an eye toward all-inclusiveness. Again Kerouac's eye focuses on the particular to render the general. Again he has Duluoz speak from above, as if he were a god, as if the identification with the eternity cited in the previous passage were complete. The omission of the apostrophe in "Seattles" (and despite Kerouac's overall irreverence for standard punctuation) is purposeful. It renders the city an emblem of many an American city. Naturally the fog, mentioned twice, indicates the haziness reminiscent of Joan Rawshank's movie set in *Visions of Cody*. As Kerouac catalogs the things of this world, he chooses seamy details: "burlesque," "cigars and wines," mundane images of "ferries," "bacon and eggs and toast." Then he sums it all up in the clause after the dash: "sweet cities below." The eye of the narrative's movement is down, and thus he descends.

The word "Down" in fact begins the following paragraph as Kerouac's eye now descends to the timber line, the specific Ponderosas, and inclusive "all-trees." The next image is a technicolor "green" and "blue." His own path is contrasted with the "cutting" boat, which is going to "beat" and "swing." The juxtaposition of the two movements allows for a tentative release in enlightenment as "candles" correspond with "souls" at the point of reaching a "there" that is the bottom. Once again, he must descend to ascend.

Looking upward, Duluoz compares this portion of the journey by stating that the last half mile is worse. But this journey down the mountain is a metaphor for Kerouac's life as a whole. Just as Duluoz laments " 'It never ends!' " the "But" signals a change in the course of the narrative. The suffering trail as "a Samsara-World-of-Suffering trail, subject to time and space, therefore must end," but it will "never end." He resolves to stop the "running" and "thwapping," lateral movements which obstruct his fall. And so, in letting go, he "falls."

But again, the contrasting movement of the boat cuts his fall short: " 'Cant make it.' " The boat represents an aspect of civilization that deters man from his descent/ascent. It represents stoppage as the narrator must "sit," "moody faced" and "finished." The "But" signals a shift in the narrative, time and civilization drawing near. The all-inclusive image of the railroad is seen in "making it"/ "not making it" on time. "It"—both civilization and time— is like a relief sculpture etched into eternity, "blasted" by society's heroes, by "Poseidon," "Zen Saints," "Master Frenchgod." Against this image of stasis, Duluoz pushes "up." But his effort to engrave himself on this surface "wont work," and he falls further—"plah."

The next paragraph is replete with christological images of the "fall." Duluoz is "loading," "placing topheavy things," feeling "strain." He is raw with "bare feet," "torn skin," "blisters," "blood," "I fall on my knees." But after a brief rest, his expression turns toward contemporary civilization, as Fred hoots and whistles to him. In keeping, then, with the antithetical imagery throughout the description, the fall from grace is balanced by the "cowboy book," "I dont want him to hear me cry," "timber tinker . . . plopping," and "wild flowers"—in short, by the civilization he has just described.

The final bridge of the passage contrasts "I cant make it" with "Gotta make it" and interprets the return to civilization as Duluoz images the descent from the mountain not in Christian terms but in a red neon imprint. The image is reminiscent of the lighting in the Hector's Cafeteria scene of *Visions of Cody* and is summed up in the haiku at the end with its "hard" mountain echoed by the clumsy line "To come down off of." And yet, the quotidian images produce the divine as well as the mundane. The movement of the journey down the mountain likens Duluoz not only to a drunk, but also to a man on his knees, seeking repentance. Hence the all-inclusive image of beat/beatitude is complete.

But the pretext of closure in the all-inclusive imagery of beat/beatitude presents a paradox. The haiku at the end suggests that we must repeat in order to progress. Thus a spiral upward is created even as Kerouac preaches a "digging deep," a down movement in the language itself. The language and structuring of language is indeed well-suited to the function of a novel that mediates, or attempts to mediate, the highly subjective quality of the experiments of *Visions of Cody* with the need to express something objective to the world. Hence the texture of Kerouac's language explains why his role as writer/self—distanced, itself an object of the novel rather than its subject—is so necessary in this book at this stage of legend. Therefore a preoccupation with expression emerges as a thematic motif in "Desolation in the World," which becomes the object of the quest that finally gives context to Duluoz's arduous journey.

Thus in section 97 the overt concern is with the problem of expression. The passage is both consistent in movement with previously cited passages and shows the characteristic progression of techniques—from general to particular and all-inclusive imagery—to resolve the paradox of beat/beatitude:

So we go out and get drunk and dig the session in the Cellar where Brue Moore is blowing on tenor saxophone, which he holds mouthpieced in the side of his mouth, his cheek distended in a round ball like Harry James and Dizzy Gillespie, and he plays perfect pretty harmony to any tune they bring up— He pays litte attention to anyone, he drinks his beer, he gets loaded and eye-heavy, but he never misses a beat or a note, because music is his heart, and in music he has found that pure message to give to the world— The only trouble is, they dont understand.

For example: I'm sitting there on the edge of the bandstand right at Brue's feet, facing the bar, but head down to my beer, for modesty of course, yet I see they dont hear it— There are blondes and brunettes with their men and they're making eyes at other men and almost-fights seethe in the atmosphere— Wars'll break out over women's eyes—and the harmony will be missed— Brue is blowing right on them, "Birth of the Blues," down jazzy, and when his turn comes to enter the tune he comes up with a perfect beautiful new idea that announces the glory of the future world, the piano blongs that with a chord of understanding (blond Bill), the holy drummer with eyes to Heaven is lilting and sending in the angel-rhythms that hold everybody fixed to their work— Of course the bass is thronging to the finger that both throbs to pluck and the other one that slides the strings for the exact harmonic key-sound— Of course the musicians in the place are listening, hordes of colored kids with dark faces shining in the dimness, white eyes round and sincere, holding drinks just to be in there to hear— It augurs something good in men that they'll listen to the truth of harmony— Brue has nevertheless to carry the message along for several chorus-chapters, his ideas get tireder than at first, he does give up at the right time—besides he wants to play a new tune— I do just that, tap him on the shoe-top to acknowledge he's right— In between the sets he sits beside me and Gia and doesnt say much and appears to pretend not to be able to say much— He'll say it on his horn—

But even Heaven's time-worm eats at Brue's vitals, as mine, as yours, it's hard enough to live in a world where you grow old and die, why be dis-harmonious? (*DA*, 198–99)

The bridge tells us the all-inclusive imagery here is harmony/disharmony, itself the image of a circle, or wholeness, especially as it pertains to musical form. Throughout the passage, images of harmony are juxtaposed with images of disharmony, up until the final question posed at the passage's end. Yet the passage is also self-reflexive in its generalization of the musician's work to stand as a metaphor for the work of any artist; it is about the ability of art—in Kerouac's particular case, of writing—to render perfection.

Echoing the movement of passages cited earlier, Duluoz will "fall" or descend in order to ascend. He will "dig" in the "Cellar." Images of harmony follow in the shape of a circle leading to perfection: "mouth" and "round ball" lead to "perfect pretty harmony"—"to any tune they bring up." He goes down, in other words, to go up. Getting "loaded" and "eye-heavy"—images of plodding like Duluoz's difficult trip down the mountain—are used to describe the travail of the musician in Kerouac's cast of types or generalized personae. The "but" is not a rhetorical contradiction but a synthesis that completes the circle of his attributive perfection—"he never misses a beat," "music is his heart." Music is his vehicle of perfection. He has found in music "that pure message to give to the world." Like Duluoz, he has a message. But, to complete the image, there is inevitably the contrast of trouble, or disharmony, stated in the negative in contrast with the prior affirmative: "they dont understand"; that is, there is no enlightenment.

"For example" is a narrative shift into the scene that follows, creating first a still setting shattered by disharmonious images. Duluoz sits facing the bar (like facing the Void) followed by a "but" that implies the synthesis of all-inclusive imagery that will emerge momentarily ("head down"). "Yet" shows the narrative will take another turn. "I see they dont hear it" shows a complete disharmony of the senses. The eyes of the people are darting about unlike the heavy eyes of those working.

Images of disharmony ensue with particular pungency in phrases like "almost-fights seethe in the atmosphere," "Wars'll break out," and "harmony will be missed."

After the dashes, images of harmony show what this audience will miss: " 'the Birth of the Blues' "—reminiscent of Kerouac's prebirth bliss—"down jazzy," that is, in "Deep Form"[7] (in its suggestion of "digging deep"). "Turn" underscores the change in narrative course as upward images make Duluoz ascend to an apocalyptic image: "up," "perfect beautiful new idea that announces the glory of the future world." This beatific view precipitates the "chord of understanding." These "up" images of "holy," "eyes to Heaven," "lilting and sending in the angel-rhythms" that cause the stillness of passing through hold everybody "fixed." And "of course" there is "the exact harmonic key-sound," the highest point. And "of course," too, the listeners who do hear—other musicians and black children described in antithetical images of "dark," "shining," "dimness," and "round"— are, unlike their down counterparts, capable of perfection themselves. The message provides a quiet apocalyptic view—"It augurs something good in men that they'll listen to the truth of harmony."

"Nevertheless" indicates another narrative turn, a lateral movement or development of the idea of carrying the message. Duluoz does so in "chorus-chapters" (his kinship and identification with the jazzman is explicit). And, wishing to progress, he continues to carry his message, to play a new tune. The lateral or shifting movement of antitheses is even graphic in "between," "beside," and "appears to pretend not to be able to say much— He'll say it on his horn."

The bridge therefore has resonance as an image of the condition of the man with the truth, with a message to convey, whether by words or music or both. In his characteristic juxtaposition of images, Kerouac creates a vision of a heaven with a landscape of hell. The disharmonious is stated in the negative, which, as we might expect by now, only serves to reinforce the positive, the affirmation of the perfection of harmony. Therefore, as writer/self, Duluoz understands his calling. Like the jazzman he must proclaim this truth of harmony through his art.

Passing Through

The second book of *Desolation Angels,* "Passing Through," was written much later than the first book and shows Duluoz experiencing the lessons of that prior "desolation." "Passing through" becomes a metaphor for traveling and, later on, a metaphor for life itself. More to the point of Kerouac's writing, "passing through" becomes a structural metaphor as it leads to the collapse of antithetical imagery in favor of images of stasis. These provide a more secure spiritual context for Kerouac's belief. Section 15 of "Passing Through Mexico" is particularly resonant in echoing the technique:

So, as Lazarus walks thru villages, so God walks thru our lives, and like the workers and the warriors we worry like worry-warts to straighten up the damage as fast as we can, tho the whole thing's hopeless in the end. For God has a bigger foot than Lazarus and all the Texcocos and Texacos and Mañanas of tomorrow. We end up watching a dusk basketball game among Indian boys near the bus stop. We stand under an old tree at the dirtroad crossing, receiving dust as it's blown by the plains wind of the High Plateau of Mexico the likes of which none bleaker maybe than in Wyoming in October, late October . . .

p.s. The last time I was in Teotihuacan, Hubbard said to me "Wanta see a scorpion, boy?" and lifted up a rock— There sat a female scorpion beside the skeleton of its mate, which it had eaten— Yelling "Yaaaah!" Hubbard lifted a huge rock and smashed it down on the whole scene (and tho I'm not like Hubbard, I had to agree with him that time). (*DA*, 244)

First, we find the general in the particular, especially in the anecdote recounted in the postscript. There is also the customary "So" transition. And there is also the characteristic antithetical movement of rhetorical tropes. But more evident here are the images of "passing through." "Walking thru," for instance, is contrasted with images of stoppage like the "worker" and "worrywarts" fixing "the damage," the still-life description of the Indian boys playing, the bus stop, and the activity of standing while the dust is blown by the winds. The hint of closure in the repetition of "end" contrasts with the abrupt cut-off line. Finally, the postscript remembrance is the concrete evidence of the message of "above," told in up/down opposition as Hubbard lifts the rock (reminiscent of Sisyphus?) and then smashes it down on the whole scene. The image of the female scorpion's murder and cannibalism of her mate is the recognition that "the whole thing's hopeless in the end." In nature the best and worst of circumstances are alike contained. There is, however, harmony and agreement in the incorporation of despair, because "passing through" is ultimately a metaphor for living life in the acceptance of its totality, bliss and despair together.

When Duluoz passes "through America again," it is to return to the realization of the perfected image. The circle is now the image of life and death together. Section 84, the last section of the novel, repeats the structural solution of the entire novel, bringing it all full circle:

So I go downtown and get an expensive hotel room to make up for it— But a sinister Marble Hotel it is— Now that Gaines' gone away all Mexico City is a sinister Marble Hive— How we continue in this endless Gloom I'll never know— Love, Suffer, and Work is the motto of my family (Lebris de Keroack) but seems I suffer more than the rest— Old Honeyboy Bill's in Heaven for sure anyway— Only thing now is Where's Jack Going?— Back to Florida or New York?— For further emptiness?— Old Thinker's thought his last thought— I go to bed in my new hotel room and soon fall asleep anyway, what can I do to bring Gaines back to the dubious privilege of living?— He's trying his best to bless me anyway but that night a Buddha's born to Gina Lollobrigida and I hear the room creak, the door on the dresser creaks back and forth slowly, the walls groan, my whole bed weaves like I say "Where am I, at sea?" but I realize I'm not at sea but in Mexico City— Yet the hotel room is rocking like a ship— It's a giant earthquake rocking Mexico— And how was dying, old buddy?— Easy?— I yell to myself "*Encore un autre petrain!*" (like the sea storm) and jump under the bed to protect myself against falling ceilings if any— *Hurracan* is whipping up to hit the Louisiana coast— The entire apartment building across the street from the post office on Calle Obregon is falling in killing everybody— Graves leer under Moon pines— It's all over.

Later I'm back in New York sitting around with Irwin and Simon and Raphael and Lazarus, and now we're famous writers more or less, but they wonder why I'm so sunk now, so unexcited as we sit among our published books and poems, tho at least, since I live with Memère in a house of her own miles from the city, it's a peaceful sorrow. A peaceful sorrow at home is the best I'll ever be able to offer the world, in the end, and so I told my Desolation Angels goodbye. A new life for me. (*DA*, 365–66)

First, a linguistic analysis reveals the repetition of the all-inclusive imagery, and second, a thematic analysis reveals the relationship of the section to the Duluoz myth. Once again the rhetorical "so" leads into the piece from the previous passage. The movement is down: "downtown" and "sinister" culminate in "endless Gloom"—the concept of gloom, in other words, has no closure. By contrast, the active tropes of "Love, Suffer, and Work" are what Duluoz inherits too: "I suffer more than the rest." This proclamation leads him to question his direction. The upward "Heaven" contrasts with Florida and New York, which can provide only "emptiness." The closure of "Old Thinker's thought his last thought" slides into images of the grave. The "bed" and "room" further signify falling—"fall asleep," "the dubious privilege of living." The attempt to bless is cut by "but" and an image of rebirth ensues ("Buddha's born"). The two movements of beat/beatitude are, in other words, once again juxtaposed with one another—"creaks back and forth," "walls groan," "bed weaves" (Kerouac's version of Whitman's cradle "endlessly rocking"). The "yet" signifies a synthesis with "room is rocking like a ship."

As this death fantasy makes Duluoz envision his own death, he begins to talk to himself, the images becoming more active than those in life. He yells and jumps and protects himself from "falling ceilings." Even a hurricane "whips" and "hits." An entire apartment building falls and kills everybody as a prologue to the final announcement that signifies closure, or the end—"It's all over" the contrast to "passing through."

"Graves leer under Moon pines" is, however, the most powerful image of the circle of closure/nonclosure. That "graves"—the image of the inanimate final resting place— are personified by "leer" and then juxtaposed with enduring images in nature—"Moon pines"—is a contrast to "It's all over," which finishes the paragraph. But not surprisingly, it does not finish the book. The final paragraph is fraught with active oppositions: "Later," "back," "more or less," "but," "sunk," "unexcited," "tho," "I live," "it's a peaceful sorrow," "in the end," "A new life for me."

Of course the creation of this language extends the Kerouac myth, and this final section of *Desolation Angels* draws the Duluoz legend to its close in the core group of Kerouac's novels. The characters (the Desolate Angels Bill Gaines, Irwin, Simon, and Lazarus) are identified by stock epithets or leitmotifs. In fact, they are deindividuated as characters in the traditional sense and reinvented as figures of myth. Bill Gaines, for example, is elsewhere called "Old Guru Gaines, in fact the first of many characters I was to know from that innocent time to now" (*DA*, 223). And "Gaines was the now fairly famous character who stole an expensive overcoat every day of his life for twenty years in New York and pawned it for junk, a great thief" (*DA*, 225). If the characters of *The Town and the City* are philosophical archetypes and those in *On the Road* and *Visions of Cody* "holy" or spiritual archetypes, here they are "angels" and godmen in fuller service to beatitude. Kerouac's mock-heroic progresses from that in his first novel. Comic types thus proliferate:

"Everybody in the world is an angel, Charley Chaplin and I have seen their wings" (*DA*, 66); W. C. Fields is conjured as a voice in a vignette involving the "Thirties Luncheonette" (*DA*, 107); and Duluoz waits for his friends in Mexico, sitting on the edge of his rooftop, "looking down on the street for the Four Marx Brothers to come walking down Orizaba" (*DA*, 231). The four principal characters are thus placed within a larger mythic and relentlessly American context.

But their main function is to put the deeply reflective narrator in relief by contrast to them. Unlike the narrator of the earlier works, this Jack Duluoz is most concerned with a self-conscious appraisal of the writer—that is, himself—as he allows life to pass through him as he passes through it in God's image. Thus the God-reflexive/self-reflexive state becomes an aspect of the development of Kerouac's mind as he advances closer to carrying out his own aesthetic philosophy of simultaneity. Duluoz says, "My life is a vast inconsequential epic with a thousand and a million characters—here they all come, as swiftly as we roll east, as swiftly the earth rolls east" (*DA*, 12).

The moon becomes the chief icon for the new level of consciousness revealed by this novel. Duluoz repeatedly invokes the moon as if it were a poetic muse: "And that night I see the Moon, Citlapol in Aztec, and even draw a picture of it on the moonlit roof with house paint, blue and white" (*DA*, 228). Thus the moon is connected integrally with the act of writing: "I remember, that is to say, a spasm takes place in my memory chamber of the brain (O hollow moon!)" (*DA*, 60). The Moon represents a category of belief in the writer/self: ". . . and over such a text as the Lankavatara Scripture which says things like . . . *Life is like the reflection of the moon on the water, which one is the true moon?* meaning: Is reality the unreal part of unreality? or vice versa, when you open the door does anyone enter or is it you?" (*DA*, 349). This passage supports the life/death theme at the end ("graves leer under Moon pines"). The moon is a circle on one plane and therefore as a shape echoes the shape of the entire work.

The circle also maintains the musical analogy by containing as well the "big rhythmic loops" that allow Kerouac to incorporate even the images that are most ugly and despairing to him:

Because by far the sweetest gift on earth . . . leads to children who are torn out of the womb screaming for mercy as tho they were being thrown to the Crocodiles of Life—in the River of Lives—which is what birth is. . . . [F]or every Clark Gable or Gary Cooper born, with all the so called glory (or Hemingway) that goes with it, comes disease, decay, sorrow, lamentation, old age, death, decomposition—meaning, for every little sweet lump of baby born that women croon over, is one vast rotten meat burning slow worms in graves of this earth. (*DA*, 267–68)

The image of rebirth is a circle that is repeated in the final pronouncement "A new life for me." Clearly the return to prebirth bliss is the goal of Kerouac's ultimate journey and his discontent in the world. He writes, "All I remember is that before I was born there was bliss" (*DA*, 283). Presumably, the ultimate circle is the return to that bliss, in death. The return to that memory of prebirth bliss is the final expression of the Duluoz legend, the end/not-end. The canonical novels—*The Town and the City, On the Road, Visions of Cody* and *Desolation*

Angels—represent the fullest expression of the life/legend and the spiritual development that completes the story they tell, even as the story remains without end.

Desolation Angels is a refinement of Kerouac's aesthetic philosophy. The circle analogy and musical metaphor go far to explain the culmination of control achieved in *Desolation Angels,* still written spontaneously as if in one long breath out of a horn but refined by a sensibility that understands the repetition of chord changes as a perpetual opportunity for refinement and revision. Thus *Desolation Angels* can be seen as the perfection of Kerouac's nonlinear or free prose. And this structural ideal underscores a thematic perfection he seeks as the object of his mythic quest.

6

Paradise Lost:
The Myth and Design of Legend

I am beginning to see a vast Divine Comedy of my own based on Buddha—on a dream I had that people are racing up and down the Buddha Mountain, is all, and inside is the Cave of Reality.

Jack Kerouac

My work comprises one vast book like Proust's except that my remembrances are written on the run instead of afterwards in a sick bed. . . . I call [the book] *The Duluoz Legend*. . . . The whole thing forms one enormous comedy, seen through the eyes of poor Ti Jean (me), otherwise known as Jack Duluoz, the world of raging action and folly and also of gentle sweetness seen through the keyhole of his eye.

Jack Kerouac
Preface to Big Sur

KEROUAC'S CRITICS to date have been content with a chronological discussion of the Duluoz legend novels, as if chronology alone could determine a

The first epigraph has been taken from a manuscript page of "Daydreams for Ginsberg," dated 10 February 1955, which is a part of the Columbia University Archives Ginsberg Collection.

literary career. Kerouac's own thoughts on the matter suggest another overall structure to the work—a wider amplification of the intrinsic structures of the language based on the jazz model. Indeed, the jazz motif suggests a structure or design that reveals the interrelationships at work in Kerouac's entire oeuvre. Now that I have delineated and explicated the core novels of the Duluoz legend, what remains is the integration of the extracanonical texts into Kerouac's "one vast book."

The core novels—*The Town and the City, On the Road, Visions of Cody, Desolation Angels*—define the development and refinement of Kerouac's style. The analogy with the musical mode has suggested that this core grouping is a frame for legend, a structure from which all the other novels can be seen as variations, both linguistically and thematically. To a greater or smaller degree, the novels of the noncanonical group—that is, all the books listed in Charters's chronology that have not yet been explicated in this study—exemplify some function (if not others) of the oscillating linguistic design already identified as characteristic of Kerouac's style and subject.[1] The novels are, to return to Allen Ginsberg's phrase, shaped as "modalities of consciousness." Each exemplifies a repetition of certain properties of the legend, with the mode of telling marking the significant change. Not only does this concept explain Kerouac's notion of revision as quite literally a repetition of seeing (as the writer's imagination and memory go back over the past to redefine it). It also allows us to see the structure of the legend as a whole.

Theme and variation allow Kerouac a structural freedom, but again the freedom has a structure of its own. The goal, as I have explored it in the core novels, is the quest for spiritual ascension, which is repressed in the oscillation of up and down movements. While the progression of the core novels is based upon this repression, some of the extracanonical works achieve the ascension repressed elsewhere. The tropes that have portrayed Kerouac's preoccupations in the canonical novels are, as I have shown, structured like mirror opposites. The extracanonical *Dr. Sax* and *Visions of Gerard* exemplify this schematization—indeed, hypostatize the characteristic oppositions at the expense of other concerns—and so represent the antithetical tropes that in turn have produced Kerouac's childhood. These novels achieve a nightmare/Christian paradise symbology, carefully hidden in the texture of *On the Road.*[2]

In other of the extracanonical novels, the ascension is achieved as an aspect of language refinement. For example, *The Subterraneans* and *Tristessa* both exemplify Kerouac's preoccupation with a love motif in a mode that succeeds only liturgically. These novels resolve a quest posed at an earlier point in the legend, again in *On the Road.*[3]

Still others of the extracanonical novels—interesting in their own right—such as *The Dharma Bums* ([1957], 1968) and *Lonesome Traveler* (1960), achieve only limited success at presenting the realization of Kerouac's style, because the overall form becomes more important than the texture of the work. The journey motif of *The Dharma Bums* or *Lonesome Traveler,* for example, repeats the road metaphor and repeats the idea of learning as one goes on, especially in the Zen overtones and teachings of the former and the hitchhiking of the latter.

The extracanonical works demonstrate the familiar antithetical emotive properties suggested by the plan of

Kerouac's major canon, exemplified, as I have shown, in the oscillation of "Beat/Beatitude": of "dream/Reality"; "racing up and down"; "comedy/tragedy"; "raging action and folly"/"gentle sweetness." These secondary works fall into two groups, which can be called "Lost Bliss" and "Bliss Achieved."

Lost Bliss

In Charters's chronology, *Dr. Sax* and *Visions of Gerard* represent novels depicting Kerouac's boyhood in Lowell, Massachusetts. While this is true, the two books can more profitably be seen as companion novels, the earliest articulations of Kerouac's preoccupation with lost bliss as first cited chronologically in *On the Road*.[4] The deep structure of Kerouac's process digs back further to explore the notion of innocence, retelling Kerouac's childhood vision, but written finally in adulthood. As companion novels, each presents the oscillating tropes or antithetical images set up and repressed within the narrative of *On the Road,* but these narratives tease out the antitheses into separate works which mirror one another. A narrative thread emerges from the core group toward a thematic and linguistic ascension.

Kerouac's experiments in narrative design continue to solve emotive problems. *Dr. Sax,* for instance, deals with Kerouac's childhood in Lowell and was written during a visit to William Burroughs in Mexico City in 1952. Both Tytell and Charters provide some discussion of the language. Tytell claims that the novel "continues the experimentalism of *Visions of Cody* with the baroque quality of its convoluted and deliberately archaic prose," while

Charters thus describes the writing: "The sentences in *Doctor Sax* rolled in long orchestrated crescendos, as if Jack were a medium for his subconscious with his mind dictating to the pencil as it traveled over his notebook pages much as he imagined Blake and Yeats had been inspired in writing their poetry."[5] Indeed, the language owes much to Kerouac's *Book of Dreams*—both being surreal, bleak, distended, and suffused with expressions of guilt. But seen in tandem with *Visions of Gerard*, this language becomes a thread pulled out of the linguistic properties of *On the Road*, explored for stylistic variation. An examination of this linguistic thread, together with the language of passion in *The Subterraneans* and *Tristessa*, will complete my discussion of this venue of Kerouac's ultimate design in the creation of a language of mythic ascension.

The linguistic oscillation of *Dr. Sax* is immediately apparent in a focused examination of an exemplary paragraph:

Doctor Sax I first saw in his earlier lineamants in the early Catholic childhood of Centralville—deaths, funerals, the shroud of that, the dark figure in the corner when you look at the dead man coffin in the dolorous parlor of the open house with a horrible purple wreath on the door. Figures of coffinbearers emerging from a house on a rainy night bearing a box with dead old Mr. Yipe inside. The statue of Ste. Thérèse turning her head in an antique Catholic twenties film with Ste. Thérèse dashing across town in a car with W. C. Fieldsian close shaves by the young religious hero while the doll (not Ste. Thérèse herself but the lady hero symbolic thereof) heads for her saintliness with wide eyes of disbelief. We had a statue of Ste. Thérèse in my house—on West Street I saw it turn its head at me—in the dark. Earlier, too, horrors of the Jesus Christ of passion plays in his shrouds and vestments of saddest

doom mankind in the Cross Weep for Thieves and Poverty—
he was at the foot of my bed pushing it one dark Saturday
night (on Hildreth & Lilley secondfloor flat full of Eternity
outside)—either He or the Virgin Mary stooped with phosphorescent profile and horror pushing my bed. That same
night an elfin, more cheery ghost of some Santa Claus kind
rushed up and slammed my door; there was no wind; my
sister was taking a bath in the rosy bathroom of Saturday
night home, and my mother scrubbing her back or tuning
Wayne King on the old mahogany radio or glancing at the
top Maggie and Jiggs funnies just come in from wagon boys
outside (same who rushed among the downtown redbricks of
my Chinese mystery) so I called out "Who slammed my
door . . ." and they said nobody . . . and I knew I was haunted
but said nothing; not long after that I dreamed the horrible
dream of the rattling red livingroom, newly painted a strange
1929 varnish red and I saw it in the dream all dancing and
rattling like skeletons because my brother Gerard haunted
them and dreamed I woke up screaming by the phonograph
machine in the adjoining room with its Masters Voice curves
in the brown wood— Memory and dream are intermixed in
this mad universe. (*DS*, 4–5)

Again Kerouac uses the by now familiar technique of
description (generalization from the particular detail)
and the rhetoric of linguistic oppositions (up and down)
that become characteristic of the books examined in the
earlier part of this study. The first sentence in the passage from *Dr. Sax* is awkward. The object of description
comes first and is followed by the statement of vision,
"I first saw"; then comes the general statement of the
"lineaments" or structures that Kerouac wishes to break
apart, a breakage accomplished by the structural solution embodied in *On the Road*. "Catholic childhood of
Centralville" follows the thematic departure of the entire
legend, evoking the ethos of innocence. But after the

dash, Kerouac enumerates dark, gloomy images which oppose the positive aspects of Catholicism and childhood: "deaths," "funerals," "shroud," a triad of negative images, underscored by the "figure in the corner," "the coffin," "the dolorous parlor," the "open house" opposed by its portal decorated with a "horrible purple wreath."

Once again Kerouac gives us an all-inclusive image containing figures in relief reminiscent of the manner of description of Hector's Cafeteria in *Visions of Cody.* The figures of the coffin bearers accentuate the sketch of the dead Mr. Yipe and the only other figure, "Ste. Thérèse," a statue or icon. This image is juxtaposed with that of a comic, highly animated film personage such as might inhabit the films of W. C. Fields—as a religious hero performing antics rather than miracles or heroic acts, heading for "saintliness" with "wide eyes of disbelief." The antithetical imagery here suggests that, for Kerouac, we respond to religion and its symbols by questioning rather than accepting. As the narrative turns, so do expectations.

Antithesis, contrast, irony, and paradox all contribute to Kerouac's technique of creating oscillating imagery in the texture of his prose, in *Dr. Sax* as in his other fiction. The next description in the quoted passage is rendered in the manner of a Biblical or religious tract where some mortal is visited by a supernatural personage (St. Joan, for example, or St. Catherine). But instead of some divine instruction of belief, it is disbelief that is emphasized through the image of the turned head—the darkness. Rather than the enlightenment that usually accompanies mystical experience, this darkness signifies a turn away from religion to "horrors," which he recounts in the suggestion of Christ in "passion" plays, a pun on the verve and slapstick of W. C. Fields, and the mention of costumes connoting "saddest doom mankind in the Cross Weep for Thieves and Poverty."

Kerouac sets this scene on an interior stage with "Eternity" outside. Kerouac's theology here places religion at the microcosm, relieved by space outside. This claustrophobic view has the image of Christ or the Virgin Mary stooped with "phosphorescent" or phony light compared to the illuminated light in which secular images bask in Kerouac's descriptions. Nightmare fantasies follow. He tells the mystery of the "cheery ghost" who rushes up and slams the door, even while mother and sister are busy elsewhere in the house. He calls out, "Who slammed my door," which is followed by a response in the negative resulting in Kerouac's recognition that he is haunted; he then tells another horrible dream from memory with skeletons that are animated. He recalls Gerard, whose memory causes him to awaken screaming in a dream within a dream. In the adjoining room a phonograph with "Masters voice" sings as in a choir to complete the churchlike but scary vision: "Memory and dream are intermixed in this mad universe."

Dr. Sax is thus a surreal vision, a vision befitting mystical experience. In *Dr. Sax,* the horrible side of Kerouac's Catholicism invades the landscape of his hometown as he explores his nightmares. Lowell becomes a symbolic Eden where all original beliefs remain intact. To return there is to return to the solid, innocent ideology of childhood learned at mother's knee, before experience, before travel. But Catholicism harbors childish terrors that are imagined through the theoretical oscillations that I have shown in *Dr. Sax. Visions of Gerard* may be seen as the positive antithesis to this negative.

The language of *Visions of Gerard* completes the picture by projecting a fantasy from the perspective of a child, with the naïveté of a saint's life. Told from the viewpoint of a younger, four-year-old brother, the book relates how Gerard died at the age of nine, only to be hallowed as a household icon. Charters finds it the earliest book in the legend, "Kerouac's earliest memories of childhood."[6] But the novel also works as the spiritual side of the fantasies of *Dr. Sax*. Written after the influence of Gary Snyder and the teachings of Buddha had assuaged the cruel disappointments of Kerouac's Catholicism, the language is elegiac, coherent, suffused with images of hope and redemption. Allusions to both Christ and Buddha abound and cause Charters to claim that Kerouac conceived *Visions of Gerard* as a "holy book."[7] But if *Dr. Sax* can be seen as portraying the dark, gloomy side of Kerouac's postfall evil, then *Visions of Gerard* presents a tainted good, or what Tytell calls its "sweet reserve of implacable resignation."[8]

As part of the postfall myth, however, each novel exemplifies aspects of the other in the linguistic correspondence with the legend. Of the fears and terrors of *Gerard*, Tytell sees, "not the fears of death—always a desired release for Kerouac—but of bondage to pain."[9] There is thus a vision of this world as the antithesis of a more positive otherworld, a paradise lost.

The following correlative scene from *Visions of Gerard* will be discussed in tandem with the previously cited passage from *Dr. Sax*:

Gerard Duluoz was born in 1917 a sickly little kid with a rheumatic heart and many other complications that made him ill for the most part of his life which ended in July 1926, when he was 9, and the nuns of St. Louis de France Parochial School were at his bedside to take down his dying words because they'd heard his astonishing revelations of heaven delivered in catechism class on no more encouragement than that it was his turn to speak——Saintly Gerard, his pure and tranquil face, the mournful look of him, the piteousness of his little soft shroud of hair falling down his brow and swept aside by the hand over blue serious eyes——I would deliver no more obloquies and curse at my damned earth, but obsecrations only, could I resolve in me to keep his fixed-in-memory face free of running off from me——For the first four years of my life, while he lived, I was not Ti Jean Duluoz, I was Gerard, the world was his face, the flower of his face, the pale stooped disposition, the heartbreakingness and the holiness and his teachings of tenderness to me, and my mother constantly reminding me to pay attention to his goodness and advice——Summers he'd lain a-afternoons, on back, in yard, hand to eyes, gazing at the white clouds passing on by, those perfect Tao phantoms that materialize and then travel and then go, dematerialized, in one vast planet emptiness, like souls of people, like substantial fleshy people themselves, like your quite substantial redbrick smokestacks of the Lowell Mills along the river on sad red sun Sunday afternoons when big scowling Emil Pop Duluoz our father is in his shirtsleeves reading the funnies in the corner by the potted plant of time and home——Patting his sickly little Gerard on the head, "*Mon pauvre ti Loup,* me poor lil Wolf, you were born to suffer" (little dreaming how soon it would be his sufferings'd end, how soon the rain, incense and teary glooms of the funeral which would be held across the way in St. Louis de France's cellar-like basement church on Boisvert and West Sixth).

For me the first four years of my life are permeant and gray with the memory of a kindly serious face bending over me and being me and blessing me——The world a hatch of Duluoz Saintliness, and him the big chicken, Gerard, who warned me to be kind to little animals and took me by the hand on forgotten little walks. (*VG,* 7–10)

The first unit of writing or introductory trope is a long-winded, intertwining motif of birth and illness that is a premonition of death and revelation. Little Gerard is explained by his own short life of nine years in one long breath, "born in 1917," "sickly," "rheumatic heart," "life ended in July 1926," with the nuns taking down his every word. Then, after a dash, Gerard's name is repeated, this time joined to the epithet "Saintly." The description that follows is eerie, ghostly: he is "mournful," "tranquil," "piteous," his hair a soft "shroud." Notice that the transition to this description follows from "his turn to speak"; now his shroud of hair is "swept aside by the hand." The movement is indicated by the strokes. Then, after a dash and in apposition to Gerard himself, is "I." But "obsecrations" are revealed instead of revelations. These are to "keep his fixed-in-memory face free of running off from me," a transition. After the next dash, this "I" explains its identity through the assertion of Gerard over the negation of Ti Jean Duluoz. A description of Gerard's face as "world," "flower," "stooped," "heartbreaking," "holy," and "tender" leads into the oracle of their mother who originated this duplicity, or this assertion of the me/not me.

Then, after the characteristic dash, Kerouac develops Gerard's vision through a description suggesting otherworldliness: the "white clouds," "Tao phantoms," and the "materialize"/"dematerialize" contrast precipitating "emptiness, like souls of people," a negative mirror image of otherworldliness. This vague imagery is set against a background of Kerouac's characteristic tropes of building: "redbrick smokestacks," which are juxtaposed, as we might expect, with images of collapsing: "sad red sun Sunday afternoons," with father "scowling" at the funnies, near the solid structure of the Kerouac hearthside, "by the potted plant of time and home." After the dash, follows the image of the child suffering and passing finally into a dream marked by the triad of "rain, incense, and teary glooms" of funerals.

"Passing Through" as a trope may be most apparent in *Desolation Angels,* but it acts here as a mode of transition of consciousness in life/death, of Duluoz's identification with the dying/dead child. He sees the first four years of his life as having been "permeant" and "gray with memory" of the face; these images act in a triad of movement: "bending over me," "being me," "blessing me." The thought is, therefore, optimistic in the suggestion of contrition. Gerard engenders a gentleness, hatching "Duluoz Saintliness."

Thus in the comparative analyses of passages from *Dr. Sax* and *Visions of Gerard* we see a composite of qualities and themes integral to Kerouac's notion of "Lost Bliss." Kerouac's imagined ideal can be seen as a "paradise lost," or a childlike vision of wonders innocent of the horrors pictured instead. In view of the Duluoz legend, this "lost bliss" may indeed signify the world that Sal Paradise sought to recover.

Bliss Achieved

For Kerouac, ascension is achieved in the refinement of the "lost bliss" theme we have just observed—especially at the level of language. The tones of *The Subterraneans* and *Tristessa* become liturgical as they begin to satisfy the quest motif; thus is "bliss achieved"—albeit temporarily.

The Subterraneans and *Tristessa* serve as variations on the courtly theme expressed in *On the Road* in the knight/squire relationship of Dean and Sal. The hero of *The Subterraneans* is aptly named Percepied, a conglomerate for a certain level of perception—digging, piercing—which becomes the goal of the quest. The language is that of an emerging consciousness, of the burgeoning underground scene of both New York and San Francisco. Percepied needs a guide to this urban terrain. He thus becomes the squire in service to his knight, in the figure of the woman called Mardou. *Tristessa* presents an analogous situation in that the heroine—ennobled in Kerouac's view to the status of Madonna—is literally a heroin addict and can be said to exist at a certain level of perception to which the narrator aspires.

These relationships as expressed in Kerouac's language reflect the romantic tendencies of the Kerouac persona, steeped as they are in the traditional affects of courtly love. The emerging persona of the Kerouac narrator experiences love sickness and total absorption in the love object. In both novels, in fact, the language is heightened to dramatize the agony of the love object and the lover.

The critic George Dardess argues that *The Subterraneans* is the earliest realization of Kerouac's style[10] of working nonstop on a novel until finished, refusing afterwards to revise his language. Tytell agrees that "the great virtue of *The Subterraneans* is its manner, its style." He further recognizes the influence of music on the writing: "[A] passage builds on improvised digressions as jazz does, using what blues players call 'landmarks,' repeated images that help to unify, and 'scat calling,' using the voice as an instrument."[11]

According to Charters's chronology, *The Subterraneans* was written in October of 1953 in three nights and published in 1958, recreating the period of the summer of 1953.[12] Kerouac specializes in the conventional form of the novel in his portrayal of the romance theme. Like *Tristessa,* it is all at once a long narrative discourse, a set of vignettes, a series of dramatic monologues in free prose, a flow of language off a central theme, a novella in its length.

The thematic consistency is provided by the voice of Leo Percepied, who most clearly embodies the sensibility of "the outsider" as inspired by Dostoyevsky's Underground Man. This voice allows Kerouac to explore the roots of Mardou's blackness, as well as his weird estrangements and attraction to addicts. The novel could be considered a fictive counterpart to Norman Mailer's essay "The White Negro" and, as such, can be seen to flesh out the description of the beat personality in its evolution from the white man who emulates the black man in the late forties, early fifties.

The jazz environment of the novel provides the perfect correspondence between literary style and the world it attempts to represent. For example, the novel recreates the sad sounds mentioned as a point of narrative in *On the Road.* In using this mode of discourse, Kerouac was practising what it was like quite literally to sing the blues, and he found the perfect example of what he considered to be a blues theme in the character of Mardou and the jazz environment.[13] The circular motif, indeed, allows Kerouac the desired integration of the blues form with a literary aesthetic.

The blues influence, moreover, allows Kerouac an artistic control over his spontaneous flow that is tighter in

The Subterraneans than passages of jazz club description in the core novels already discussed. Mardou and her urban setting provide a linguistic model, as Neal Cassady had in the characters of Dean Moriarty and Cody Pomeray. The Kerouac persona, Leo Percepied, acts as Mardou's squire, to maintain the relationship of the elegiac romance through which the Sal and Dean friendship is defined in *On the Road*. Here, Kerouac is so fascinated by the speech of the black girl that he, according to Charters,

succeeded in taking the way the girl spoke, her syntax and her style, and added his own interpolations and private thoughts which he put down simultaneously with her monologues and their conversations. The sentence structure had broken through to include private thoughts just above the level of consciousness, and yet it had the sound of American actual speech, all welded together by the muscular force of Jack's prose energy.[14]

The single paragraph in which Kerouac describes a jazz party at the Red Drum illustrates a controlled style of generalizing from the particular and the collapse of antithetical imagery to display beat/beatitude:

So there we were at the Red Drum, a tableful of beers a few that is and all the gangs cutting in and out, paying a dollar quarter at the door, the little hip-pretending weasel there taking tickets, Paddy Cordavan floating in as prophesied (a big tall blond brakeman type subterranean from Eastern Washington cowboy-looking in jeans coming in to a wild generation party all smoky and mad and I yelled "Paddy Cordavan?" and "Yeah?" and he'd come over)—all sitting together, interesting groups at various tables, Julien, Roxanne (a woman of 25 prophesying the future style of America with short almost crewcut but with curls black snaky hair, snaky walk, pale pale junky anemic face and we say junky when once Dostoevski would have said what? if not ascetic or saintly? but not in the least? but the cold pale booster face of the cold blue girl and wearing a man's white shirt but with the cuffs undone untied at the buttons so I remember her leaning over talking to someone after having slinked across the floor with flowing propelled shoulders, bending to talk with her hand holding a short butt and the neat little flick she was giving it to knock ashes but repeatedly with long long fingernails an inch long and also orient and snake-like)—groups of all kinds, and Ross Wallenstein, the crowd, and up on the stand Bird Parker with solemn eyes who'd been busted fairly recently and had now returned to a kind of bop dead Frisco but had just discovered or been told about the Red Drum, the great new generation gang wailing and gathering there, so here he was on the stand, examining them with his eyes as he blew his now- settled-down-into-regulated-design "crazy" notes—the booming drums, the high ceiling—Adam for my sake dutifully cutting out at about 11 o'clock so he could go to bed and get to work in the morning, after a brief cutout with Paddy and myself for a quick ten-cent beer at roaring Pantera's, where Paddy and I in our first talk and laughter together pulled wrists— now Mardou cut out with me, glee eyed, between sets, for quick beers, but at her insistence at the Mask instead where they were fifteen cents, but she had a few pennies herself and we went there and began earnestly talking and getting high-tingled on the beer and now it was the beginning—returning to the Red Drum for sets, to hear Bird, whom I saw distinctly digging Mardou several times also myself directly into my eye looking to search if really I was that great writer I thought myself to be as if he knew my thoughts and ambitions or remembered me from other night clubs and other coasts, other Chicagos—not a challenging look but the king and founder of the bop generation at least the sound of it in digging his audience digging his eyes, the secret eyes him-watching, as he just pursed his lips and let great lungs and immortal fingers work, his eyes separate and interested and humane,

the kindest jazz musician there could be while being and therefore naturally the greatest—watching Mardou and me in the
infancy of our love and probably wondering why, or knowing
it wouldn't last, or seeing who it was would be hurt, as now,
obviously, but not quite yet, it was Mardou whose eyes were
shining in my direction, though I could not have known and
now do not definitely know—except the one fact, on the way
home, the session over the beer at the Mask drunk we went
home on the Third Street bus sadly through night and throb
knock neons and when I suddenly leaned over her to shout
something further (in her secret self as later confessed) her
heart leapt to smell the "sweetness of my breath" (quote) and
suddenly she almost loved me—I not knowing this, as we
found the Russian dark sad door of Heavenly Lane a great
iron gate rasping on the sidewalk to the pull, the insides of
smelling garbage cans sad-leaning together, fish heads, cats,
and then the Lane itself, my first view of it (the long history
and hugeness of it in my soul, as in 1951 cutting along with
my sketchbook on a wild October evening when I was dis-
covering my own writing soul at last I saw the subterranean
Victor who'd come to Big Sur once on a motorcycle, was
reputed to have gone to Alaska on same, with little subterranean chick Dorie Kiehl, there he was in striding Jesus coat
heading north to Heavenly Lane to his pad and I followed
him awhile, wondering about Heavenly Lane and all the long
talks I'd been having for years with people like Mac Jones
about the mystery, the silence of the subterraneans, "urban
Thoreaus" Mac called them, as from Alfred Kazin in New
York New School lectures back East commenting on all the
students being interested in Whitman from a sexual revolu-
tion standpoint and in Thoreau from a contemplative mystic
and antimaterialistic as if existentialist or whatever standpoint,
the *Pierre*-of-Melville goof and wonder of it, the dark little
beat burlap dresses, the stories you'd heard about great ten-
ormen shooting junk by broken windows and starting at their
horns, or great young poets with beats lying high in Rouault-
like saintly obscurities, Heavenly Lane the famous Heavenly
Lane where they'd all at one time or another the beat

subterraneans lived, like Alfred and his little sickly wife something straight out of Dostoevski's Petersburg slums you'd think
but really the American lost bearded idealistic—the whole
thing in any case), seeing it for the first time, but with Mardou,
the wash hung over the court, actually the back courtyard of
a big 20-family tenement with bay windows, the wash hung
out and in the afternoon the great symphony of Italian mothers, children, fathers BeFinneganing and yelling from step-
ladders, smells, cats mewing, Mexicans, the music from all the
radios whether bolero of Mexican or Italian tenor of spaghetti
eaters or loud suddenly turned up KPFA symphonies of Vivaldi harpsichord intellectuals performances boom blam the
tremendous sound of it which I then came to hear all the
summer wrapt in the arms of my love—walking in there now,
and going up the narrow musty stairs like in a hovel, and her
door. (*S*, 18–22)

First the transitional "So" indicates connection with
the narration thus far; then, the location of the Red
Drum is established with a small description of the scene.
The verbs in the present participle ("cutting," "paying,"
"pretending," "taking," "floating,") indicate the continued action as part of Kerouac's creation of an all-inclusive effect; the movement includes the opposing "in and
out." Within the parentheses, Paddy Cordavan is described, not merely mentioned, but as a caricature (isolated like Joan Rawshanks in *Visions of Cody*), a radiant
portrait of every time Percepied has ever seen him
there—a "big blond brakeman type"—a proletarian image augmented by his position as subterranean. Kerouac
recounts their typical encounter and associates him with
an American type in the epithet "cowboy-looking." The
phrase "all sitting together" is in apposition to the first
phrase and reestablishes the location after the brief
digression, arcing the narration in a small circle.

"All" signals the following word flow. The name "Roxanne" intones another digression of description within parentheses, establishing yet another American type, prophetic of "the future" and attributed with Eden-like images of evil in the repetition of "snaky." But then this "snaky" quality is ennobled as Kerouac characteristically brings the image full circle. He attributes the anemic junky with the qualities of a Dostoyevskian "possessed" character (a reminder of "the Holy Goof" of *On the Road*), who would be seen ironically as "ascetic or saintly." But the attribution is given as a question, the affirmation qualified by "but" and rhetorical antithesis. "Girl" is set in juxtaposition with "man"; her movement is associated with the snake ("slinked") and rendered in the present participle ("leaning," "talking," "flowing," "bending," "holding," "giving"). "Snake-like" brings all full circle.

Another location phrase set in apposition to those already cited, "groups of all kinds," brings the description back rhetorically for another small circle of narration. The narrative thus spirals "up" to the stand where the musician, Charlie Parker, is (unlike the horn player in *On the Road,* who simply creates "IT") characterized by the figures of courtly love—that is, his "solemn eyes" suggest a correspondence with "bop dead Frisco." The repetitions of the club, the group, and Bird on the stand provide another small narrative circle until the eye movements bring us back to him, his "crazy" notes "now-settled-down-into-regulated-design," just as Kerouac's narrative is now revealed to be so settled.

In the mention of the "high ceiling," Kerouac attributes the qualities of a church or cathedral to the club. "Adam" recalls the Eden-like suggestions in the Roxanne description. But this characteristic Kerouacean heightening of mundane images builds to the introduction of Mardou, the object of both the vision and the adoration—"the beginning." The "cut out" to get beers cheaper at the Mask is their first "glee-eyed" adventure, "earnest" and "hightingled."

The phrase "returning to the Red Drum for sets," signals a shift to a new spiral of narration, bringing the action forward by including new tropes for the music of Bird, whose eyes are now digging Mardou. The word "digging" evokes the "Deep Form" recommended in Kerouac's critical essays and in a previously noted passage in *Desolation Angels.* "Digging" provides for a synaesthesia of sound and sight recalling a technique of experimentation in *Visions of Cody.* Moreover, "the secret eyes" conjure images through which love of the courtly kind is realized. An adoring description of physical features—"lips," "lungs," "fingers"—in operation as Bird plays suggests that in nature, or in the creation of natural sounds, he is "humane," "great," and "immortal," in short, the "greatest," the "king." But the observer, Percepied, receives these images and is recharged by a reflected image in the jazz player; he identifies with him through their mutual interest in the woman, but also in their mutual fascination as artists, the jazzman a mirror of the writer in the imagined correspondence of thoughts: "as if he knew my thoughts and ambitions or remembered me."

This discourse appropriately shifts to Mardou. The tentativeness of the description, suggested by the conditional clauses led by "though" and "except." These clauses indicate the particular obsession or love sickness that characterizes Percepied's fascination with his love object, "whose eyes were shining in his direction," and underscores the courtly quality of this love. The overlay of spiritual imagery becomes as obsessive as the characteristic, corresponding contrary imagery introduced in the phrase "except the one fact."

And just as Bird has been seen as the "kindest," "immortal," "king," the eyes shift from his image to Mardou. She now becomes a symbol of "the infancy of our love." The ennobling innocence of this thought is undercut, however, by the bus trip home, which shows the contrasting imagery: "sadly through night," "throb knock neons." The turning point of this large narrative circle design is the heightening/diminishing of the love in both Percepied and Mardou. Enlightenment is diverted by "neons," as Percepied misses to perceive: "she almost loved me—I not knowing this." Indeed, Percepied's missing to perceive causes the down-cycle. A failed moment of bliss has occurred in her "secret self," she "later confessed" (a word charged with heavy Christian overlay), as "her heart leapt." Yet Percepied misses the perception and with it concomitant grace.

A down movement ensues in smaller up and down spirals. "Heavenly Lane" has a "dark sad door," "a great iron gate" that rasps on the "sidewalk to the pull." The "insides of smelling garbage cans sad-leaning together, fish heads, cats" indicates the rude underside to this "Heaven." A new locating phrase now brings the narrative back: "my first view of it." As we might expect, a long parenthetical description of "it" turns out to be the discovery of "my own writing soul," sparked by Heavenly Lane, despite the rudeness of its images. The description parallels that in the jazz club: tropes of "digging," "subterraneans," the geography of America. The subterranean as saintly recalls a parallel description of an up movement, this time the "Jesus coat." The Christian overlay is seen further in images of "silence" and "mystery." Then the existential "urban Thoreaus" are juxtaposed with the contemplative and mystical American transcendentalists: this vision heaps Alfred Kazin with Melville, Thoreau, Whitman in an oblique association of "the American lost bearded idealistic" with "Dostoevski's Petersburg slums." These "saintly obscurities" developed within the digression are completed by "the whole thing in any case."

Once again the narrative shifts to Mardou; the locating phrase brings us back with "seeing it for the first time." This time she is seen in the negative. "But" turns our attention to the martyred image of "the wash hung over the court," "actually the back courtyard . . . with windows,"—a panel of vision like relief sculpture on a frieze. These visual images are followed by the aural images of a cacaphony, a "symphony," complete with many ethnic and animal sounds, of "mothers," "fathers," "children," "Italian," "Mexican," "music from all the radios," and "cats mewing"—all the sounds one might hear in a city courtyard. In juxtaposition with this urban sonata is the music of Vivaldi symphonies, the sounds of "harpsichord intellectuals." The confused images mirror Percepied's love affair with Mardou. He is now "walking in"—literally "going up" and spiritually ascending toward enlightenment through love. But again, as we might expect by now, the "narrow musty stairs" lead to "a hovel," to "the door" to her apartment of love, and also to the next narrative circle.

The paragraph from *The Subterraneans* thus accomplishes Kerouac's desired simultaneity of representation through a complicated iconography. His details and images are drawn through memory and imagination in the customary contrasts of courtly ideals/homely images of everyday life. Lofty images of Catholicism and Western culture counter images of daily reality. In *Tristessa,* he goes even further to reveal the highs and lows, the up and down, the pleasure and pain of love, both secular and spiritual, as the same, all-contained.

Tristessa exemplifies the development from the language of the blues as seen in *The Subterraneans* to the language of passion. Passion, in the medieval sense, signifies a confluence of sexual excitement and religious fervor. Indeed, to have brought the myth of romance to the ethos of the Beat Generation in order to establish spiritual values in the fear that "everything is collapsing" (as Kerouac warns in *On the Road*) seems a higher pleasure of *The Subterraneans,* and is even more the case in *Tristessa,* where the romanticism of the Vivaldi harpsichord is developed linguistically.

The novel's history informs the linguistic development. *Tristessa* was written in a stone hovel by candlelight in Mexico City in 1955 and is a cult novel for Kerouac enthusiasts. A local prostitute named Esperanza Villanueva was the object of Kerouac's impassioned imagination, according to all accounts. Kerouac dubs his heroine Tristessa or Sadness, partly because of Esperanza's melancholy voice and partly because he saw in the affliction of the woman's drug use an illustration of the Buddhist principle that all life is suffering. In other words, the incredible high has couched within a terrible low operating dramatically and simultaneously. Kerouac was thus attracted to this voice for a literary reason; but, moreover, "Tristessa" became the object of an impossible love.

In the second half of the novel, written a year later, after Kerouac had spent the summer on Desolation Peak as a fire watcher, the tone changes. During the summer Kerouac had declared his love for "Tristessa" in letters. The tone of the second half of the novel reflects how he found her when he returned—bitter, sinister, hopelessly resigned—the style is itself muted by the picture of the woman destroyed by drugs. From this tragedy Tytell concludes that "*Tristessa* explores the holiness of the ugly and disaffiliated, and is punctuated by references to Catholic ritual and Hindu myth," but he goes on to describe only the deeper meaning in Kerouac's relationship to women as can be determined in these novels.[15] Rather than explore this element of Kerouac's biography, it is more to the purpose here to examine the nature of Kerouac's language of passion.

Tytell briefly mentions Kerouac's style; he finds the sentences much shorter than in *The Subterraneans,* with a greater emphasis on omitted articles, prepositions, and connectives, in order to capture the feeling of Tristessa's own clipped and quaint English. Tytell also recounts Kerouac's own recognition of the change in style from the earlier novel, and how, in a letter to Ginsberg, Kerouac points out the terse choppiness, pointed humor, and total elimination of the more euphemistic and flowery elements of *The Subterraneans*.[16]

Indeed, the language of *Tristessa* is liturgical. She becomes a Beatrice to Kerouac's Dante, leading the poet to Heaven. She is the linguistic counterpart to Mardou, just as Mardou had been to Dean/Cody, but she is also more ephemeral and becomes a symbol of Christianity as the language increases its hymnal tones. Here is a sample passage from part 1, ironically entitled "Trembling and Chaste":

Tristessa is sitting on the edge of the bed adjusting her nylon stockings, she pulls them awkwardly from her shoes with big sad face overlooking her endeavors with pursy lips, I watch the way she twists her feet inward convulsively when she looks at her shoes.

She is such a beautiful girl, I wonder what all my friends would say back in New York and up in San Francisco, and what would happen down in Nola when you see her cutting down Canal Street in the hot sun and she has dark glasses and a lazy walk and keeps trying to tie her kimono to her thin overcoat as though the kimono was supposed to tie to the coat, tugging convulsively at it and goofing in the street saying "Here ees the cab—hey hees hey who—there you go—I breeng you back the moa-ny." Money's moany. She makes money sound like my Old French Canadian Aunt in Lawrence "It's not you moany, that I want, it's you loave"—Love is loave. "Eets you lawv." The law is lawv. —Same with Tristessa, she is so high all the time, and sick, shooting ten gramos of morphine per month,— staggering down the city streets yet so beautiful people keep turning and looking at her—Her eyes are radiant and shining and her cheek is wet from the mist and her Indian hair is black and cool and slick hangin in 2 pigtails behind with the roll-sod hairdo behind (the correct Cathedral Indian hairdo)—Her shoes she keeps looking at are brand new not scrawny, but she lets her nylons keep falling and keeps pulling on them and convulsively twisting her feet—You picture what a beautiful girl in New York, wearing a flowery wide skirt a la New Look with Dior flat bosomed pink cashmere sweater, and her lips and eyes do the same and do the rest. Here she is reduced to impoverished Indian Lady gloom-clothes—You see the Indian Ladies in the inscrutible dark of doorways, looking like holes in the wall not women— their clothes—and you look again and see the brave, the noble

mujer, the mother, the woman, the Virgin Mary of Mexico.—
Tristessa has a huge ikon in a corner of her bedroom.

It faces the room, back to the kitchen wall, in right hand
corner as you face the woesome kitchen with its drizzle showering ineffably from the roof tree twigs and hammberboards
(bombed out shelter roof)—Her ikon represents the Holy
Mother staring out of her blue charaderees, her robes and
Damema arrangements, at which El Indio prays devoutly when
going out to get some junk. El Indio is a vendor of curios,
allegedly,—I never see him on San Juan Letran selling cru-
cifixes, I never see El Indio in the street, no Redondas, no
anywhere—The Virgin Mary has a candle, a bunch of glass-
fulla-wax economical burners that go for weeks on end, like
Tibetan prayer-wheels the inexhaustible aid from our Amida—
I smile to see this lovely ikon. . . .

I sit admiring that majestical mother of lovers. (*T*, 10–12)

Kerouac's basic stylistic innovations are evident in the
section. First, there is the direct borrowing of his subject's speech, as if he were transcribing an interview with
her (analogous to sections of *Visions of Cody*). An example
is, "I breeng you back the moa-ny." Second, there is
interlocking phrase structure: the tendency is to forgo
end- stop in favor of a circular, looping repetition of key
words and sounds that provide for the interior circles
and spirals of narrative. For example, the word "shoes"
is a leitmotif in Tristessa's characterization. Third, the
section illustrates the collapse of antithetical imagery from
beat/beatitude, the highs/lows becoming part of the same
movement as the spiritual/mundane. For example, Tristessa is seen as beautiful in contrast to her convulsive
movements—but only as beautiful as a junky in Mexico.
The image is extended by the narrator's fantasy of what
she would be like as a beautiful girl in America; in turn,
and as we might expect, the image is extended by the

"ikon" of the Virgin Mary in the corner of her bedroom. All become one in Kerouac's writer eye. Finally, the section contains the all-inclusive circular imagery of the general from the particular: the picture of Tristessa at the outset gives rise to all of the narrator's musings about his love object. For example, he spiritualizes her in the final line of adoration: "I sit admiring that majestical mother of lovers."

Now in closer detail: Up to the first end-stop there is the concrete description of Tristessa adjusting her stockings, pulling, "overlooking," sitting as her lover looks adoringly on. "Pursy," "twists," and "convulsively" suggest a less than perfect quality to her movements, and in fact betray her drug addiction. "She is such a beautiful girl" repeats the subject of the description twice, in apposition to "Tristessa" at the outset, the word "beautiful" suggesting the opposing tropes of beat/beatitude. The narrator fantasizes about his subject: he follows her movements as they are imagined in Nola—"hot," "dark," "lazy," this time tying her coat, "tugging convulsively at it." The action of "cutting down" recalls the prior action in the passage of *The Subterraneans* when Mardou and Percepied seek cheaper beer. Then the narrator mimics her sound by conjuring the image of an old aunt in Lawrence and by mixing money, love and law. The gentle tease is equated with Tristessa's perpetual high: "she is so high all the time." In fact, the crude image of the drug addict—"sick," "shooting" morphine, and "staggering"—becomes an ironic configuration of love, money, and the law.

"Yet" turns the description to another meaning of high; as "people keep turning," so does the narrator and narrative. Tristessa is now attributed with radiance, her hair a "correct Cathedral Indian hairdo." The exotic in Tristessa is thus emphasized in the elegant terms meant to contrast with the mean junky images, as if she were a religious artifact or icon herself. Especially beatific is the reference to the architecture of her hair, woven as if it were a cathedral or church. Then the narrative characteristically shifts to a repetition of the initial detail, moving downward to her feet from high—"falling," "pulling," "convulsively twisting."

By contrast, the picture of what Tristessa would be like in New York is adorned with purity: "flowery wide skirt," "pink cashmere sweater." Again, however, the narrative moves downward to "reduced to impoverished Indian gloom-clothes"; from this particular detailed study Kerouac retreats his focus to take in the whole, generalizing to all the Indian ladies and revealing their association with mystery (and sexuality): "inscrutable dark doorways," "holes in the wall," "the mother," and finally "the Virgin Mary of Mexico."

Thus spiritualized, the image becomes a transition to the following section with "Tristessa has a huge ikon in a corner of her bedroom." The sentence is a conductor into what follows: the image of women as vehicles, symbolic of, leading into, providing entrance to—in a sexual sense—"dark" "holes," a sense that includes the mysteries of religion as well. The Virgin Mary is, after all, the ultimate symbol of the purity of woman, in the Catholic church and elsewhere. While the icon intertwines this spiritual and sexual union, "El Indio prays devoutly when going out to get some junk." The image of the Virgin Mary who "has a candle" that burns "for weeks on end" and that signifies an eternal enlightenment is undercut by the "vendor of curios" who prays so devoutly before it. Like the image of the "Tibetan prayer-wheels" and the "inexhaustible," the full circle contains both the highest high and the lowest low.

"One Vast Book"

Yet, in the end, as with *The Subterraneans,* love is ephemeral and doomed to die. Both novels reflect the persistence, even obsession, of romantic idealism, that joins the language of sexual passion to that of religious passion, heightened by the representation of love as a drugged state. But even as the twelfth-century *Tristan and Isolde* instructs us, romantic love is doomed to die; it cannot be lived within society. Like the courtly women in medieval romances, Kerouac's Mardou and Tristessa in particular are symbols of inconstancy and therefore yet another reflection of his ultimate despair.

Despite the constant emotive oscillations in Kerouac's work both major and minor, his achievements overshadow his ambivalences. The interconnection in *Tristessa* of the holy icon with the bedroom is a climactic moment in Kerouac's myth. The greatest sexual and spiritual highs occur simultaneously in the mundane imagery of this room. The third paragraph of the passage from *Tristessa* clarifies this union in the juxtaposition/identity of the holy icon with the junkie who adores it. What an ironic Beatrice to Kerouac's Dante! The otherworldliness in her eyes is a matter of addiction and despair, hardly the beatitude of the church. The junkie and holy Mother facing each other in prayer, moreover, become part of the "inexhaustible," going on for weeks without end, like "Tibetan prayer-wheels"—part of the endless spiritual circle.

7

The Last Word

The only real thing about a writer is what he has written and not his so-called life.

William S. Burroughs

THE CREATION OF a new literary ethic was, in fact, the ultimate goal of Kerouac's artistic quest, and also its demise. Fiction that draws heavily on the writer's life—that is praised and not diminished for being called autobiographical—was still an innovation during Kerouac's lifetime. Part of Kerouac's anguish can surely be attributed to the fact that he was unable to see his work in print as he wished to see it, with the original names intact, and still be accepted as fiction. Kerouac was not writing in the language of history, of course, but in the language of the imagination; his creation of himself is a self writ large in the Whitmanesque sense. Similarly, while Kerouac's writing at first appears to be a critique of America and its values, there is a resolution, a romantic potential achieved in art. A national character is projected in Kerouac's singular voice: in the broader context of American literary history Kerouac conjures the Huck Finn image, the raft supplanted by the automobile, the Mississippi River replaced by the open highway.

Kerouac's distinct voice develops through the stages of his legend as defined in my study—first, the original paradise and lost innocence of Lowell, Massachusetts; second, the road as lapsed innocence and transition to the third stage, in which Kerouac embraces a Buddhist philosophy, retaining the spiritual structure of the quest despite his questioning of traditional religious values; and finally, the last stage and tragic conclusion of the Kerouac legend: its meditative retreat from society. Kerouac's desire for transcendence is ironically played out in a progressive obsession with death.

Two important works flesh out the legend as it moves from its first statements toward its emphasis in *Desolation Angels: Big Sur* and *Vanity of Duluoz.* These novels underscore an essential belief of this study—that a literary, not a historical imagination prevails in the Legend of Kerouac.

"The Sea is My Brother"

Sometime in 1942, according to Gerald Nicosia's account of Kerouac's life, Jack Kerouac wrote a novel he called "The Sea is My Brother," comprised of imitation Melvillian prose, long, bombastic sentences filled with "romantic and poetic appeciations of the sea."[1] Twenty years later the sea—specifically at Big Sur—becomes a resonant image in Kerouac's novelistic account of a nervous breakdown, *Big Sur,* as well as in its coda, an addenda of poetry entitled "Sea: Sounds of the Pacific Ocean at Big Sur." The book was written in ten nights and chronicles a six-week period in Big Sur during the summer of 1960, climaxing in a breakdown at Lawrence Ferlinghetti's cabin. The novel attests to Kerouac's obsession with death.

Death and madness are key thematic motifs; the highs and lows of Kerouac's exuberant style account for Duluoz's retreat as a reaction to literary celebrity. Duluoz is repulsed by fans expecting him to act like a "beatnik," by drunken visitors "puking in my study, stealing books and even pencils" (*BS*, 5). Realizing he was "surrounded and outnumbered and had to get away to solitude again or die" (*BS*, 5), Duluoz hitchhikes to California, goes into retreat, and goes crazy.

Kerouac's craziness is not described in the style of F. Scott Fitzgerald's "The Crack-Up," which is, after all, recounted in the rational prose we might expect from magazine reportage. By the time of the writing of *Big Sur*, Kerouac already had the techniques for his own subjective collapse in hand. Very few sentences form thoughts in this book. Instead the book is filled with dash-joined images providing a breathy, impressionistic effect, a cataloging of detail reminiscent of Whitman's "Song of Myself" and Ginsberg's "Howl":

But there's moonlit fognight, the blossoms of the fire flames in the stove—There's giving an apple to the mule, the big lips taking hold—There's the bluejay drinking my canned milk by throwing his head back with a miffle of milk on his beak— There's the scratching of the raccoon or of the rat out there, at night—There's the poor little mouse eating her nightly supper in the humble corner where I've put out a little delight-plate full of cheese and chocolate candy (for my days of killing mice are over)—There's the raccoon in his fog, there the man to his fireside, and both are lonesome for God. . . . (*BS*, 37)

The writing is encumbered by excessive language. Rather than a quest for spirituality that is suggested by an optimism, exuberance, and frequent references to Catholicism and Buddhism, there appears to be an attempt to justify his sins. This Kerouac/Duluoz retreat is quite different from the isolation of Desolation Peak. Note the following wisdom on drunkenness:

> Any drinker knows how the process works: the first day you get drunk is okay, the morning after means a big head but so you can kill that easy with a few more drinks and a meal, but if you pass up the meal and go on to another night's drunk, and wake up to keep the toot going, and continue on to the fourth day, there'll come one day when the drinks wont take effect because you're chemically overloaded and you'll have to sleep it off but cant sleep any more because it was alcohol itself that made you sleep those last five nights, so delirium sets in—Sleeplessness, sweat, trembling, a groaning feeling of weakness where your arms are numb and useless, nightmares, (nightmares of death). . . well, there's more of that up later. (*BS*, 74–5)

The end is the predictable double movement. On the one hand Duluoz proclaims: "Something good will come out of all things yet—And it will be golden and eternal just like that—There's no need to say another word" (*BS*, 216). On the other hand, in the final poetic section Duluoz is overcome by the equation of the sea with death: the "machinegun sea" (*BS*, 240); "The sea'll / only drown me" (*BS*, 232); "these waves scare me— / I am going to die in full despair" (*BS*, 233); "For me, for us, the Sea, / the murdering of time by eating / lusty cracks of lip feed wave / at aeons of sandy artistry / till nothing's left but old age" (*BS*, 236–37); "Farewell, Sur" (*BS*, 241).

The Vanity of Kerouac

"The Sea is my Brother" is a leitmotif in *Vanity of Duluoz*, Kerouac's last ambitious work. Completed in mid-May of 1967 and published in 1968, the book is written from the point of view of Jack Duluoz, who is speaking to his wife (called "wifey") in an elaborate dramatic monologue, telling her the story of his life so that she might better comprehend his present despair at, ironically, having become a successful writer. As he puts it, "For after all what is success? You kill yourself and a few others to get to the top of your profession . . . so that when you reach middle age . . . you can stay home and cultivate your own garden in bliss; but by that time . . . mobs come rushing across your garden and trampling all your flowers. What's with that?" (*VD*, 17). As we might expect, the sea once again figures in an association with death, as much an obsession in this novel as it was in *Big Sur*. In this novel, though, the accounts of Duluoz's exploits at sea become part of the plot patterning of Duluoz's professed "adventurous education of a young man," the book's subtitle in the tradition of Hemingway.

Gerald Nicosia calls *Vanity of Duluoz* the work of a "master paradoxist," finding it "funny," its humor derived of "self-parody."[2] It would be more helpful to see the self-mockery in this book as the maturity of the mock-heroic device begun with *The Town and the City*, Kerouac's first novel. In scenes depicting Thanksgiving dinner, football, war, life at sea, and the Greeks in Lowell, Massachusetts, as Homeric heroes, Kerouac revives the themes of his early work in his now mature style.

Rather than create several characters to reveal in their actions and speech the widening consciousness of the world Kerouac wished to describe in the early work, Kerouac's Duluoz narrates the tale but acts also as an intrusive commentator on events. In a reminiscence of Lowell, for example, Duluoz stops to comment, "This is the story of the techniques of suffering in the working world, which includes football and war" (*VD*, 76). Or, in a section about his studies at Columbia University, Duluoz pauses in his own version of literary criticism to pay homage to Thomas Wolfe, who "made me want to prowl, and roam, and see the real America that was there and that 'had never been uttered' " (*VD*, 56). Kerouac's experimentalism finally exhibits itself in the manner of the narrator of *Tristram Shandy*. Kerouac creates a narrative voice—in regular sentences and without the dashes—so sure of itself he will digress, talk French, link up disparate threads of his past, philosophically muse over them, and break his discourse in exhortation to his intended audience.

The most compelling part of this novel comes in the recreation of the Columbia University milieu; the catalyst for Peter's growth and awareness in *The Town and the City* here becomes dramatized and raised to the level of myth. Filled with references to Kerouac's earlier books, which unify the legend by repeating it, the tale narrated by Duluoz centers around a murder involving a character named Claude, who is possessed by a kind of "New Vision" described as Dostoyevskian, existential, inspired by Rimbaud and Nietzche, Yeats and Rilke. In a Gidean "acte gratuite," Claude kills a boy named Franz, who had been trailing Claude about. Jack Duluoz becomes an accessory to this crime and marries his sweetheart Johnnie while he is still in jail, and so on. For anyone who is unfamiliar with these events, they are a recreation of actual facts that form a scandalous part of early Beat history. What is of interest here, however, is how Kerouac integrates this story with other unresolved material and transmutes these events into myth.

Never losing touch with his essential preoccupations, Kerouac brings them into his circular design. The Duluoz tirade on birth and death shows how Kerouac has never really resolved the central question of *The Town and the City*—"What was it that had killed his father?"—as he brings it together with other questions and other deaths. There is only the passive understanding that even his questions are a vanity. Believing finally that "birth is the direct cause of all pain and death" (*VD*, 211), Duluoz can only pray for redemption:

Yet I saw the cross just then when I closed my eyes after writing all this. I cant escape its mysterious penetration into all this brutality. I just simply SEE it all the time. . . . Madmen and suicides see this. Also dying people and people in unbearable anguish. What SIN is there, but the sin of birth? (*VD*, 211)

Ha ha ha ha she's laughing as she dances on the dead she gave birth to. Mother Nature giving you birth and eating you back. . . . That's not even worse, for God's sake, than watching your own human father Pop die in real life, when you really realize "Father, Father, why hast thou forsaken me?" for real, the man who gave you hopeful birth is copping out right before your eyes and leaves you flat with the whole problem and burden (your self) of his own foolishness in ever believing that "life" was worth anything but what it smells like down in the Bellevue Morgue when I had to identify Franz's body. Your human father sits there in death before you almost satisfied. That's what's so sad and horrible about the "God is Dead" movement in contemporary religion, it's the most tearful and forlorn philosophical ideal of all time. (*VD*, 209)

And finally,

I settled down to write, in solitude, in pain, writing hymns and prayers even at dawn, thinking, "When this book is finished, which is going to be the sum and substance and crap of everything I've been thru throughout this whole gaddam life, I shall be redeemed." (*VD*, 213)

Even at end, when Duluoz raises his cup to life ("Hic calix! . . . 'Here's the chalice,' and be sure there's wine in it" [*VD*, 214]), Kerouac's imagery encompasses the contradictions of his Buddhism and Catholicism. He realizes the true end of his spiritual quest: he achieves the only solace he has ever had—as a writer writing. And in this act lies his redemption.

Paradoxically, Kerouac the writer, capable of explaining the soul through its journeys on the open road, the expansive American highway, capable of visions he identified as beatific, dies of a massive internal hemorrhage, a complication of alcoholism, incapable of preventing his own self-destruction, incapable of recognizing in his last years the tragedy that had become his life. If indeed a literary, not a historical, imagination prevails, the language of ascension that describes this down-journey and despair will remain the seminal statement of this moment in American literary history.

Notes

Bibliography

Index

Notes

Preface

1. The first biography to appear was the pioneering *Kerouac: A Biography* (San Francisco: Straight Arrow Books, 1973; reprint, New York: Warner, 1973) by Ann Charters. Charles Jarvis's *Visions of Kerouac* (Lowell, Mass.: Ithaca Press, 1975) followed with useful information about Kerouac's life in Lowell. The next— *Jack's Book: An Oral Biography of Jack Kerouac* (New York: St. Martin's Press, 1978) by Barry Gifford and Lawrence Lee—had an interesting cross-country interview strategy. The fourth was the idolizing *Desolate Angel: Jack Kerouac, the Beat Generation, and America* (New York: Random House, 1979) by Dennis McNally. The next, the massive *Memory Babe: A Critical Biography of Jack Kerouac* (New York: Grove, 1983) by Gerald Nicosia, was followed by the minimal *Jack Kerouac* (San Diego: Harcourt Brace Jovanovich, 1984) by Tom Clark. Films—both documentaries and docudramas—join proliferating reminiscences in supplying additional biographical information. Notable memoirs include Carolyn Cassady's *Heart Beat: My Life with Jack and Neal* (Berkeley: Creative Arts, 1976) and Joyce Johnson's *Minor Characters* (Boston: Houghton Mifflin, 1983).

2. Morris Dickstein, *Gates of Eden: American Culture in the Sixties* (New York: Basic Books, 1977, p. 280) cites the three sharpest attacks on the Beat writers in the earliest responses to their writing, all of which appear in *Partisan Review:* John Hollander's review of *Howl* (Spring 1957), Norman Podhoretz's "The Know-Nothing Bohemians" (Spring 1958), and Diana Trilling's "The Other Night at Columbia" (Spring 1959). Podhoretz's essay was

reprinted in his *Doings and Undoings* (New York: Farrar, Straus, 1964) and in *A Casebook on the Beat,* ed. Thomas Parkinson (New York: Thomas Y. Crowell, 1961); Trilling's piece reappeared in her *Claremont Essays* (New York: Harcourt Brace, 1964). The bulk of this criticism deals very little with the literature itself, drawing on its content as a personal attack upon conventional English expression and, in fact, using the novels as sociological rather than literary documents.

1. Introduction

1. Dickstein, *Gates of Eden,* p. 12.
2. Seymour Krim, Introduction to *Desolation Angels,* pp. ix–xxviii (New York: Putnam's, 1965), reprinted as "The Kerouac Legacy" in *Shake It for the World, Smartass* (New York: Dial, 1970), p. 195.
3. Jack Kerouac, "The Last Word," *Escapade,* June 1959, p. 72.
4. Jack Kerouac, "Essentials of Spontaneous Prose," *Evergreen Review* 2 (Summer 1958): 73, 72.
5. John Tytell, *Naked Angels: The Lives and Literature of the Beat Generation* (New York: McGraw-Hill, 1976), p. 17.
6. M. H. Abrams, *The Mirror and the Lamp* (New York: Norton, 1953), p. 224.
7. Quoted in Harold Bloom, *Poetry and Repression: Revisionism from Blake to Stevens* (New Haven: Yale Univ. Press, 1976), p. 241.
8. Ann Charters in *Kerouac: A Biography* (New York: Warner, 1973) mentions how *The Town and the City* was first published because it was reminiscent of Thomas Wolfe's *Look Homeward Angel* (p. 107); for the book's mixed critical reception, see p. 117.
9. Kerouac discusses his own language in "Essentials of Spontaneous Prose"; "Belief and Technique for Modern Prose," *Evergreen Review* 2 (Spring 1959): 57; "The Last Word"; and in "The Art of Fiction XLI: Jack Kerouac," interview by Ted Berrigan et al., *Paris Review,* 43 (Summer 1968): 61–103, rpt., in *Writers at Work: The Paris Review Interviews,* 4th Series, ed. George Plimpton, pp. 361–95. (New York: Penguin, 1974).
10. Though the term "spontaneous bop prosody" is commonly known and used, Allen Ginsberg originated the name for Kerouac's language in his dedication to *Howl* as cited in Charters, *Kerouac,* p.261; in his creative and critical essays on Kerouac's craft that appear as the introduction to *Visions of Cody* (New York: McGraw-

Hill, 1973); and in the essay entitled "Kerouac," in *Allen Verbatim,* ed. Gordon Ball (New York: McGraw-Hill, 1974), pp. 151–60.

11. Malcolm Cowley's role in the publication of *On the Road* was to have insisted upon the changes necessary to "regularize" the text. See Charters, *Kerouac,* p. 223, and Tytell, *Naked Angels,* pp. 157–158. These critics disagree on the question of whether or not Kerouac revised. Charters says he did, while Tytell claims that Kerouac did not see anything from the original to the published version.

12. See Timothy A. Hunt, *Kerouac's Crooked Road: Development of a Fiction* (Hamden, Conn.: Shoe String Press, Archon Books, 1981), for a comprehensive study of *Visions of Cody* as the fifth revision of *On the Road.* Hunt claims that "what was published in 1957 by Viking Press as *On the Road* was the fourth version" (p.xvii).

13. Charters, *Kerouac,* pp. 357, 358. Duluoz was, of course, Kerouac's fictional name for himself in several of the novels and in his conception of the legend in its entirety.

14. Charters, *Kerouac,* p. 359.

15. Columbia University Archives, manuscript pages of "Daydreams for Ginsberg," Ginsberg Collection, 10 February 1955.

16. Critics Timothy A. Hunt and Gerald Nicosia prefer to discuss Kerouac's innovative language from the point of view of "wild form," a term that Kerouac used in a letter to John Clellon Holmes written 3 June 1952. See Hunt, *Kerouac's Crooked Road,* p. 121, and Nicosia, *Memory Babe,* p. 392.

17. Tytell, *Naked Angels,* p. 146.

18. Charters, *Kerouac,* p. 358.

19. Albert Murray, *Stomping the Blues* (New York: McGraw-Hill, 1976), p. 96.

20. Kerouac, *Paris Review* interview, p. 378.

21. Warren Tallman, "Kerouac's Sound," in *A Casebook on the Beat,* ed. Thomas Parkinson (New York: Thomas Y. Crowell, 1961), p. 222.

22. Kerouac, "Essentials of Spontaneous Prose," p. 72.

23. Guy Rosolato, "The Voice and the Literary Myth," in *The Structuralist Controversy,* ed. Richard Macksey and Eugenio Donato (Baltimore: Johns Hopkins Univ. Press, 1970), pp. 209–10.

24. Leo Marx, in *The Machine in the Garden: Technology and the Pastoral Ideal* (New York: Oxford Univ. Press, 1964), describes and evaluates the uses of the pastoral ideal in the interpretation of the American experience.

25. Tytell, *Naked Angels,* p. 141.

26. Gertrude Stein's essay on repetition, in *Lectures in America* (Boston: Beacon Press, 1957), pp. 165–206, makes clear the importance of incremental repetition and the ever present "now" in the truly American utterance.

27. Charters, *Kerouac*, p. 358.

2. The Brothers Martin or the Decline of America

1. Hermann Hesse, "The Brothers Karamazov, or the Decline of Europe" 1919, rpt. in *My Belief: Essays on Life and Art*, ed. Theodore Ziolkowski (New York: Farrar, Straus, and Giroux, 1974), pp. 70–85.

2. Tytell, *Naked Angels*, pp. 63–64.

3. See Harold Bloom, *The Anxiety of Influence: A Theory of Poetry* (New York: Oxford Univ. Press, 1963).

4. From the first reviews on, critical analyses have sought these imitative qualities, as if establishing a lack of originality could actually tell readers something about the talent—or lack of it—in its creator. For a review of the general reception to *The Town and the City*, see Charters, *Kerouac*, pp. 117–118, and Tytell, *Naked Angels*, p. 149.

5. A representative selection of Thomas Wolfe criticism can be found in Louis Rubin, ed., *Thomas Wolfe: A Collection of Critical Essays* (Englewood Cliffs: Prentice-Hall, 1973).

6. Quoted in Charters, *Kerouac*, p. 61.

7. Bloom, *The Anxiety of Influence*, pp. 82–83.

8. See chapter 1, note 9 above for the citations of Kerouac's discussions of his writing philosophy.

9. Charters, *Kerouac*, p. 65.

3. The Road as Transition

1. Kerouac, "Belief and Technique for Modern Prose," p. 57.

2. Tytell, *Naked Angels*, p. 63.

3. Dorothy Van Ghent, "Comment," in *A Casebook on the Beat*, ed. Thomas Parkinson, p. 213.

4. See Kenneth A. Bruffee, *Elegiac Romance: Cultural Change and Loss of the Hero in Modern Fiction* (Ithaca: Cornell Univ. Press, 1983).

5. See Sigmund Freud, *Beyond the Pleasure Principle*, trans. James Strachey (1920; reprint, New York: Norton, 1961). Freud defines an instinct as "an urge inherent in organic life to restore an earlier state of things which the living entity has been obliged to abandon under the pressure of external disturbing forces" (p. 30).

6. Tytell states explicitly, "Kerouac identified Cassady with his lost brother Gerard" (*Naked Angels*, p. 62). See also my analysis of *Visions of Gerard* in chapter 6.

7. Kerouac, "Essentials of Spontaneous Prose," p. 73.

8. Charters, *Kerouac*, p. 129.

9. Quoted in Charters, *Kerouac*, pp. 127–28.

10. Tytell, *Naked Angels*, pp. 67–68.

11. Kerouac, "Belief and Technique in Modern Prose," p. 57.

12. In Gifford and Lee's *Jack's Book*, Malcolm Cowley is quoted as attesting to Kerouac's careful revision of *On the Road*. Cowley thought that Kerouac should write in regular sentences and not as if writing were like "toothpaste coming out of a tube" (p. 206).

13. Nicosia, *Memory Babe*, pp. 352, 353, 356, 441.

14. See Tytell's discussion of *Visions of Cody* in *Naked Angels*, p. 175ff.

15. Kerouac, "Belief and Technique in Modern Prose," p. 57; Kerouac, "Essentials of Spontaneous Prose," p. 72.

16. Kerouac, "Essentials of Spontaneous Prose," p. 72.

17. For a brief analysis of Kerouac's writing in *On the Road* in tandem with his professed method of composition see LeRoi Jones, "Correspondence," *Evergreen Review* 2 Spring (1959): 253–56.

18. See Murray, *Stomping the Blues*.

19. To quote Kerouac from his essay "Essentials of Spontaneous Prose": "CENTER OF INTEREST. Begin not from preconceived idea of what to say about image but from jewel center of interest in subject of image at *moment* of writing, and write outwards swimming in sea of language to peripheral release and exhaustion" (p. 73).

20. Of course—and ironically—Kerouac is entirely paradoxical in his insistence upon writing "without consciousness." As he puts it in his essay "Essentials of Spontaneous Prose": "MENTAL STATE. If possible write 'without consciousness' in semi-trance (as Yeats' later 'trance writing')" (p. 73).

21. Kerouac explains in "Essentials of Spontaneous Prose": "Satisfy yourself first, then reader cannot fail to receive telepathic shock and meaning-excitement by same laws operating in his own human mind" (p. 72).

4. Modalities of Consciousness

1. Allen Ginsberg, "Kerouac," p. 160. Ginsberg attributes the psychological term "modality of consciousness" to Humphrey Osmond.
2. Tytell, *Naked Angels,* p. 175.
3. See Roman Jakobson and Morris Halle, *Fundamentals of Language,* (1955; reprint, The Hague: Mouton, 1971), especially the chapter on "The Metaphoric and Metonymic Poles" (pp. 90–96).
4. See Kerouac, "Essentials of Spontaneous Prose," p. 73: "If possible write without consciousness."
5. LeRoi Jones, ed., *The Moderns: An Anthology of New Writing in America* (London: MacGibbon and Kee, 1965), pp. 266–77.
6. Tytell, *Naked Angels,* p. 69. For the purposes of this discussion, the differences between "expansion" and "revision" are semantic. Hunt in *Kerouac's Crooked Road* avoids linguistic analysis but provides interesting commentary on the interrelation of the novels under discussion.
7. Ginsberg calls the book an "in-depth" version of *On the Road* (in Charters, *Kerouac,* p. 141). In his introduction to *Visions of Cody,* Ginsberg also considers the novel a "historical sequel" to *On the Road* (p. ix).
8. Walter Pater, *The Renaissance: Studies in Art and Poetry* (1873; reprint, New York: Modern Library, 1919), p. 135.
9. Allen Ginsberg considers this passage a Homeric hymn (see Ginsberg's Introduction to *Visions of Cody,* p. vii).
10. Tytell, *Naked Angels,* pp. 175–76.
11. Carolyn Cassady, *Heart Beat,* p. 27.

5. The Sound of Despair: A Perfected Nonlinearity

1. Tytell, *Naked Angels,* p. 174.
2. Krim, "The Kerouac Legacy," p. 214.
3. McNally, *Desolate Angel,* p. 295.
4. Tytell, *Naked Angels,* pp. 174, 175.
5. Quoted in Tytell, *Naked Angels,* p. 173.
6. The Columbia University Archives houses numerous manuscript pages of Kerouac's American haikus. These demonstrate his interest in a poetic form that accompanies his interest in Zen philosophy. In *Desolation Angels* his prose paragraphs often cul-

minate in haiku lines that form a "bridge" to the next section. Kerouac also mentions his interest in haiku in his *Paris Review* interview, p. 367.

7. Kerouac, "Essentials of Spontaneous Prose," p. 73.

6. Paradise Lost: The Myth and Design of Legend

1. Charters, *Kerouac*, p. 404.
2. Kerouac speaks specifically of a Shrouded Traveler, a romantic specter as yet unexplained, but heavily laden with mystical properties in *On the Road*.
3. A narrative refrain of *On the Road* is Dean's idea that "Sex is holy."
4. See *On the Road*, p. 105.
5. Tytell, *Naked Angels*, p. 187; Charters, *Kerouac*, p. 158.
6. Charters, *Kerouac*, p. 252.
7. Charters, *Kerouac*, p. 252.
8. Tytell, *Naked Angels*, p. 190.
9. Tytell, *Naked Angels*, p. 190.
10. George Dardess, "The Logic of Spontaneity: A Reconsideration of Kerouac's 'Spontaneous Prose Method,'" *Boundary* 2–3 (1975): 729.
11. Tytell, *Naked Angels*, p. 199.
12. Charters, *Kerouac*, pp. 404, 186.
13. Kerouac's preoccupation with the blues is demonstrated in his *Mexico City Blues (242 Choruses)* (New York: Grove, 1959).
14. Charters, *Kerouac*, p. 186.
15. Tytell, *Naked Angels*, p. 203.
16. Tytell, *Naked Angels*, p. 202.

7. The Last Word

1. Nicosia, *Memory Babe*, p. 103.
2. Nicosia, *Memory Babe*, p. 673.

Selected Bibliography

Publications by Jack Kerouac

The Town and the City. New York: Harcourt, Brace, 1950.

On the Road. New York: Viking, 1957.

The Subterraneans. New York: Grove, 1958.

The Dharma Bums. New York: Viking, 1958.

"Essentials of Spontaneous Prose." *Evergreen Review* 2 No. 5 (Summer 1958): 72–73.

"The Last Word (My position in the current American literary scene)." *Escapade,* June 1959, p. 72.

"Belief and Technique for Modern Prose." *Evergreen Review* 2 (Spring 1959): 57.

Doctor Sax. New York: Grove, 1959.

Maggie Cassidy. New York: Avon Books, 1959.

Mexico City Blues. New York: Grove, 1959.

Tristessa. New York: Avon Books, 1960.

Lonesome Traveler. New York: McGraw-Hill, 1960.

Scripture of the Golden Eternity. New York: Totem/Corinth, 1960.

Book of Dreams. San Francisco: City Lights, 1961.

Big Sur. New York: Farrar, Straus, and Cudahy, 1962.

Visions of Gerard. New York: Farrar, Straus, 1963.

Desolation Angels. New York: Coward-McCann, 1965.

Satori in Paris. New York: Grove, 1966.

"The Art of Fiction XLI: Jack Kerouac." Interview by Ted Berrigan et al. *Paris Review,* 43 (Summer 1968): 61–103. Reprint in *Writers at Work: The Paris Review Interviews,* 4th

Series, edited by George Plimpton, pp. 361–95. New York: Penguin, 1974.

Vanity of Duluoz: An Adventurous Education, 1935–46. New York: Coward-McCann, 1968.

Pic. New York: Grove, 1971.

Scattered Poems. San Francisco: City Lights, 1971.

Visions of Cody. New York: McGraw-Hill, 1972.

Two Early Stories. New York: Aloe Editions, 1973.

Old Angel Midnight. London: Booklegger/Albion, 1973.

Trip Trap. (Jack Kerouac, Albert Saijo, and Lew Welch.) Bolinas, Calif.: Grey Fox, 1973.

Heaven and Other Poems. Bolinas, Calif.: Grey Fox, 1977.

Secondary Sources

Abrams, M. H. *The Mirror and the Lamp*. New York: Norton, 1953.

Amram, David. *Vibrations: The Adventures and Musical Times of David Amram*. New York: Macmillan, 1968.

Bartlett, Lee, ed. *The Beats: Essays in Criticism*. Jefferson, N.C.: McFarland, 1981.

Bloom, Harold. *The Anxiety of Influence: A Theory of Poetry*. New York: Oxford University Press, 1963.

―――. *Poetry and Repression: Revisionism from Blake to Stevens*. New Haven: Yale University Press, 1976.

Bruffee, Kenneth A. *Elegaic Romance: Cultural Change and Loss of the Hero in Modern Fiction*. Ithaca: Cornell University Press, 1983.

Cassady, Carolyn. *Heart Beat: My Life With Jack and Neal*. Berkeley: Creative Arts, 1976.

Charters, Ann. *Kerouac: A Biography*. San Francisco: Straight Arrow Books, 1973. Reprint. New York: Warner, 1973.

————. *A Bibliography of Works by Jack Kerouac 1939–1975.* Revised edition. New York: Phoenix Bookshop, 1975.

Clark, Tom. *Jack Kerouac.* San Diego: Harcourt Brace Jovanovich, 1984.

Cook, Bruce. *The Beat Generation.* New York: Scribner's, 1971.

Dardess, George. "The Logic of Spontaneity: A Reconsideration of Kerouac's 'Spontaneous Prose Method.' " *Boundary* 2–3: (1975) 729–43.

Dickstein, Morris. *Gates of Eden: American Culture in the Sixties.* New York: Basic Books, 1977.

Feldman, Gene, and Max Gartenberg. *The Beat Generation and the Angry Young Men.* New York: Citadel, 1958.

Freud, Sigmund. *Beyond the Pleasure Principle.* Trans. James Strachey. 1920. Reprint. New York: Norton, 1961.

Gifford, Barry, and Lawrence Lee. *Jack's Book: An Oral Biography of Jack Kerouac.* New York: St. Martin's Press, 1978.

Ginsberg, Allen. "The Dharma Bums." *Village Voice,* 12 November 1958, pp. 3–5.

————. *Allen Verbatim: Lectures on Poetry, Politics, Consciousness.* Edited by Gordon Ball. New York: McGraw-Hill, 1974.

————. *The Visions of the Great Rememberer: With Letters by Neal Cassady and Drawings by Basil King.* Amherst, Mass.: Mulch Press, 1974.

————. *Journals: Early Fifties Early Sixties.* Edited by Gordon Ball. New York: Grove, 1977.

Hesse, Hermann. "The Brothers Karamazov, or the Decline of Europe." 1919. Reprint in *My Belief: Essays on Life and Art,* edited by Theodore Ziolkowski, pp. 70–85. New York: Farrar, Straus, and Giroux, 1974.

Hipkiss, Robert A. *Jack Kerouac: Prophet of the New Romanticism.* Lawrence, Kans.: Regents Press, 1976.

Holmes, John Clellon. *Nothing More to Declare.* New York: Dutton, 1967.

Hunt, Timothy A. *Kerouac's Crooked Road: Development of a Fiction.* Hamden, Conn.: Shoe String Press, Archon Books, 1981.

Jakobson, Roman, and Morris Halle. *Fundamentals of Language.* 1955. Reprint. The Hague: Mouton, 1971.

Jarvis, Charles E. *Visions of Kerouac.* Lowell, Mass.: Ithaca Press, 1974.

Johnson, Joyce. *Minor Characters.* Boston: Houghton Mifflin, 1983.

Jones, LeRoi. "Correspondence." *Evergreen Review* 2 (Spring 1959): 253–56.

—————, ed. *The Moderns: An Anthology of New Writing in America.* London: MacGibbon and Kee, 1965.

Knight, Arthur, and Glee Knight, eds. *the unspeakable visions of the individual* 3, nos. 1 and 2 (1973).

—————. *The Beat Book: Volume 4, the unspeakable visions of the individual.* Privately printed: California, Pa., 1974.

Knight, Arthur, and Kit Knight, eds. *The Beat Diary: Volume 5, the unspeakable visions of the individual.* Privately printed: California, Pa., 1977.

—————. *The Beat Journey: Volume 8, the unspeakable visions of the individual.* Privately printed: California, Pa., 1978.

—————. *the unspeakable visions of the individual* 10 (1980).

—————. *Beat Angels: Volume 12, the unspeakable visions of the individual.* Privately printed: California, Pa., 1982.

—————. *Dear Carolyn: Volume 13, the unspeakable visions of the individual.* Privately printed: California, Pa., 1983.

Krim, Seymour. Introduction to *Desolation Angels,* pp. ix–xxviii. New York: Putnam's, 1965. Reprint as "The Kerouac Legacy" in *Shake It for the World, Smartass,* pp. 193–216. New York: Dial, 1970.

Lawrence, D. H. *Studies in Classic American Literature.* New York: Viking, 1923.

Mailer, Norman. *The White Negro*. Reprint. San Francisco: City Lights, 1957.

Marx, Leo. *The Machine in the Garden: Technology and the Pastoral Ideal*. New York: Oxford University Press, 1964.

McClure, Michael. *Scratching the Beat Surface*. Berkeley: North Point Press, 1982.

McNally, Dennis. *Desolate Angel: Jack Kerouac, the Beat Generation, and America*. New York: Random House, 1979.

Milewski, Robert J. *Jack Kerouac: An Annotated Bibliography of Secondary Sources, 1944–1979*. Metuchen, N. J.: Scarecrow Press, 1981.

Miller, Henry. *The Colossus of Maroussi*. New York: New Directions, 1941.

———. Preface to *The Subterraneans*. New York: Avon Books, 1958.

Murray, Albert. *Stomping the Blues*. New York: McGraw-Hill, 1976.

Nicosia, Gerald. *Memory Babe: A Critical Biography of Jack Kerouac*. New York: Grove, 1983.

O'Brien, John, ed. *Review of Contemporary Fiction* 3 (Summer 1983). Kerouac/Pinget Issue.

Parkinson, Thomas, ed. *A Casebook on the Beat*. New York: Thomas Y. Crowell, 1961.

Pater, Walter. *The Renaissance: Studies in Art and Poetry*. 1873. Reprint. New York: Modern Library, 1919.

Pearce, Roy Harvey. *The Continuity of American Poetry*. Princeton: Princeton University Press, 1961.

Rosolato, Guy. "The Voice and the Literary Myth." In *The Structuralist Controversy*, edited by Richard Macksey and Eugenio Donato, pp. 209–10. Baltimore: Johns Hopkins University Press, 1970.

Rubin, Louis, ed. *Thomas Wolfe: A Collection of Critical Essays*. Englewood Cliffs: Prentice-Hall, 1973.

Saroyan, Aram. *Genesis Angels: The Saga of Lew Welch and the Beat Generation.* New York: William Morrow, 1979.

Stein, Gertrude. *Lectures in America.* Boston: Beacon Press, 1957.

Tytell, John. *Naked Angels: The Lives and Literature of the Beat Generation.* New York: McGraw-Hill, 1976.

Walsh, Joy, ed. *Moody Street Irregulars: A Jack Kerouac Newsletter,* nos. 1–11 (1978–1982).

Wyse, Seymour. Interview by Dave Moore. *The Kerouac Connection: Beat Brotherhood Newsletter,* nos. 3–6 (July 1984–April 1985).

Index

Regina Weinreich has a B.A. from Brooklyn College, an M.A. from the University of Wisconsin at Madison, and a Ph.D. from New York University. She has been on the faculties of Brooklyn College, Rutgers University, and New York University. She has published widely in periodicals including the *New York Times Book Review,* the *Review of Contemporary Fiction, Village Voice, Omni,* and *Soho News.* She has cowritten a documentary film on the Beat Generation and currently teaches "Experimental Writing" at The School of Visual Arts, New York City.